Understanding Kazuo Ishiguro's

A complete GSCE Study Guide for GCSE English Literature students for exams from 2017.

By Gavin Smithers

Another of Gavin's Guides- study books packed with insight. They aim to help you raise your grade! This guide is intended as a study aid for GCSE students and their teachers who are preparing for GCSE exams in 2017 and subsequent years.

It will also be helpful for A level students who read the novel as part of their extended reading. The novel is popular in many schools for coursework at A level.

Series Editor: Gill Chilton

Cover Photo: Robin Wright

The complete text of "Never Let Me Go" is published by Faber and Faber. You will need a copy of the text to use and refer to alongside this guide.

Published by Gavin's Guides. All rights reserved. No part of this publication may be reproduced or transmitted in any form or by any means, electronic or mechanical, including photocopy, recording or any information storage and retrieval system, without the prior written permission of the publisher. Copyright Gavin Smithers, 2017. The right of Gavin Smithers to be identified as the author of this work has been asserted in accordance with the Copyright, Designs and Patents Act 1988. This book is copyright material and must not be copied, reproduced, transferred, distributed, leased, licensed or publicly performed or used in any way except as specifically permitted in writing by the publishers, as allowed under the terms and conditions under which it was purchased or as strictly permitted by applicable copyright law. Any unauthorized distribution or use of this text may be a direct infringement of the author's and publisher's rights and those responsible may be liable in law accordingly.

CONTENTS

A unique story – and how to study this book 4

Your exam – what you are expected to do 6

Attention AQA candidates 8

Attention OCR candidates 9

Attention WJEC candidates 9

Introduction to the novel – an overview, plus some ideas and issues... 11

The film adaptation – and a caution 13

Rebellion and conforming 14

Structure and narrative organisation 19

The 'Big Brother' Society 23

Commentary and analysis:

Chapters 1 to 23..28

The main characters and where to find them:

Kathy H 104

Tommy D 108

Ruth 111

Madame 114

Miss Emily 115

Major themes 116

The importance of fear.............................. 117

Friendship 118

Intimacy 119

Death 121

The role of hope 122

The importance of memories 124

How to do exam questions 125

Sample essays:

AQA style 127

WJEC style 129

Appendix

Timelines 133

Chronology...137

A note on names 153

A unique story – and how to study this book

This novel was first published in 2005. It was shortlisted (and, unofficially, the runner-up) for the prestigious Man Booker prize. It now features as an option in the modern prose category for English Literature GCSE with three of the exam boards- AQA, OCR and WJEC.

Ishiguro has established his position over the last 35 years as one of our most admired contemporary literary novelists. "Never Let Me Go" appears, at first, to be quite child-like in its writing style, but your detailed study of it should enable you to show that there is real depth just beneath the surface. The narrator is a young woman limited, as well as defined, by what she has experienced, and also by the experience she has lacked.

By traditional standards, there is little in the way of plot- two trips to seaside towns, and one to see a stranded boat on a beach. But there is a great deal of dramatic tension, as the pitiless conditions and terms of the characters' lives gradually become clear. The reader is required to piece together and connect what is already connected in Kathy's thoughts. Perhaps the most troubling part of the puzzle is the fatalistic acceptance she and all her friends apply to what they know about their futures, once the "fantasy" of a deferral is destroyed, with nothing to soften it.

The novel will leave you considering how you would live the remainder of your life, if you knew approximately when you would die. What would you make of the life you have lived and the people you have known? What would you value? Possessions? Friendships? Solitude?

It will also set you thinking about why we take so little interest in technology and science, unless it is our profession. Why do we allow people we neither know nor communicate with- politicians, and scientists- so much freedom to set the parameters of our lives? Are we content that the least powerful are protected from abuses of power; and, if not, what are we prepared to do about it?

There is a useful film adaptation of the novel, starring Carey Mulligan, Andrew Garfield and Keira Knightley and distributed by Fox. The novel runs to almost 300 pages; the film runs for 99 minutes. It is the equivalent of the highlights of a football match; very different from witnessing the whole event.

Read the novel, slowly and carefully, at least twice; doing that, and using this guide to help you, will give you a very strong basis for sitting your exam with confidence.

Becoming a careful reader means that you will find *connections, echoes and clues* throughout; this will help you to see the hidden skills in the narrative. You will then both enjoy and admire the story all the more- and have a solid platform, when you write essays about the themes, and, more importantly, the meaning of the novel.

You should therefore be ready to say what you find in it; and this should be different from what I or your teachers find in it, because we all read differently. Our own experience and temperament are individual to us, and we cannot ignore those influences when we read this- or any other- novel.

The one thing readers of this particular novel will share, though, is a sense of gratitude at having had the opportunity to read it and study it.

Students of Hailsham feel that they have had a privileged time there; reading this novel somehow manages to leave the reader with the sense that reading about their world is a kind of privilege too.

After you have done this, you will not see your own world in quite the same way- and that, in the end, is the purpose of any worthwhile art or literature.

Your exam- what you are expected to do

You will be aware that GCSE exams have undergone great change. The first exams under the new specifications are those that you may be preparing for, in the summer of 2017. Depending on the exam board, the format and the emphasis of the exam question will vary slightly, but the aim is always broadly the same for GCSE.

You will not be allowed to take a copy of the text into the exam.

This means that the first hurdle is to have a clear and close understanding of the plot and the structure of the novel.

Ishiguro helps by making the structure of his novel straightforward. The book is divided into three parts- set first at Hailsham, until the characters are aged 16, then at the cottages, and then in the world of carers and donors. Kathy's memories are given to us in a jumbled way which requires us to sort and organise them. Think of this as doing a jigsaw puzzle. At the end of this guide, I have set out the historical order of events, to make it clearer for you.

GCSE exam questions are designed to be fair, and to give you the opportunity to show that you have studied the novel, thought about it, and come to understand how and why you respond to it as you do. Any text selected for GCSE will have the potential to make us think in new ways about some aspects of our own lives. When you have read "Never Let Me Go", you should be able to make a list of the questions it raises in your own mind. Then you can work out what it is in the novel which has been thought-provoking for you.

"Never Let Me Go" is a good example of a novel where the author has been specific about the issues he intends to raise, and his reason for writing it- to explore what matters to us once we become conscious that the reminder of our life is a short time span.

When the novel was published, its author was aged 50 – an age when many adults begin to reflect on the pattern of their lives. Younger readers will have a different outlook, and so the key issue is for you to be clear what the novel is saying *to you*.

For AQA candidates, your task is to write one essay (from a choice of two) as part of Paper 2; 20% of your overall mark is at stake. You should allocate 45 minutes to this task. The exam board is looking for you to show your critical skills in reading and comprehension; you need to distinguish between the literal narrative and what it implies or infers, and to deduce the meaning of the novel- what it says to us- from what is in it (its action). You will have the opportunity to demonstrate that you have thought about the novel's themes, considered how other readers may respond to them, and that you can analyse and explain your own personal response, with quotations or references which show where that comes from.

You should be able to explain how Ishiguro uses vocabulary, grammar and structure to create meaning.

The assessment objectives for this essay are mainly AO1, which tests how closely you have read and understood the novel and how well you can explain and support your own view of what it has to say to its readers; and AO2, which requires you to show that you can explain how the meaning of the novel comes from its language, form and structure.

AQA essay questions tend to be broadly based, offering you a theme which you can relate to your understanding of the whole text.

If your exam board is OCR, the question will be slightly different, but the work you produce will contribute potentially 25% of your overall marks. The assessment objectives are, not surprisingly, designed to reward you for giving an informed personal response to the text, using the architecture of the novel- its themes and ideas, characters and relationships, language, form and structure- to arrive at and set out your opinion of its meaning.

In addition to writing specifically on "Never Let Me Go", the OCR exam involves comparing an extract from the novel with an extract from an unseen text which will share some similar themes and contexts; there are marks, under AO3, for how well you manage this comparison.

WJEC candidates will earn 20% of their overall GCSE from writing for an hour on this text in Unit 2A. You are required to spend twenty minutes writing about a short passage (usually, but not necessarily, to analyse the mood and atmosphere) and forty minutes writing an essay, which may be about one of the main characters (Kathy, Tommy, Ruth) and/or their relationships. Or you may be invited to give your own view on an interpretative judgment- for example, that the novel is about "the steady erosion of hope", or that it is "dark and upsetting".

Examiners' reports stress that you must not rely on the film version of the novel; **you are being examined on the text of the novel, not the film.**

The marking scheme focuses on AO1 and AO2, and also on AO4. Your response needs to show evidence of a critical and imaginative personal response to the novel, with textual references which support your point of view. You must be able to show how the language, structure and form of the novel present its themes and ideas. An awareness of context is needed- in this case, the question of the scientific and moral basis of the novel.

To summarise-

All exam boards are trying to give you a fair chance to show that you have read the novel carefully and that you have thought about it. What is unusual about it? It is rare to find young people living in a pitiless society which will kill them not long after the age of 30. We see the characters in that light. Their lives have been different from ours. Do we recoil from them because they are clones? Or do we admire them? Feel sorry for them? Feel frightened of them?

What do we like and dislike about them? And what effect does their story have on us? In what ways does the novel make us reconsider our own ambitions, priorities and behaviour?

Introduction to the novel – an overview, plus some ideas and issues

That Ishiguro's novel is so prominent in the GCSE specifications indicates that it offers opportunities to find hidden meanings below the surface of its story, and that it stimulates readers to consider some important questions.

In this guide, we will explore those themes- including the ethics of science and human rights, perceptions of intimacy, and the position of minorities.

Kazuo Ishiguro was born in Japan but grew up in England from the age of 5. He attended a boys' grammar school and went on to study English and Creative Writing at the Universities of Kent and East Anglia.

His family spoke Japanese at home but he considers his literary influences as non-Japanese. He has said that his upbringing gives him a rather different and distinctive perspective as a writer.

Ishiguro has given numerous written and video interviews, which are accessible on the internet. Regarding this particular novel, he has said that the science/eugenics are not, for him, the core issue. He asks us to enter into the emotional world of young characters who **accept their fate**, and refuse to run away from it, because they do not have the perspective- or social vision- to rebel against it.

He says that he is interested in the role of love and friendship in our lives, in the context of the constant, but usually anaesthetised, awareness we have in the back of our minds that our lives are finite- that we will all die.

By making his characters' lives so sharply abbreviated- none of them can live beyond their mid-thirties- he heightens the fact that, sooner, for many people (faced, for example, with terminal illness), and for all of us, at some point, this awareness of our own impending death must become intense.

One consequence of this is that we will tend to evaluate our relationships, and, in Kathy's case, we "order" our memories, so that, when we face our own death, we do so with some consolation from the life we have lived.

This is a different experience from that of those who do not have families.

In a sense, we all face the end of our lives alone; but, for Ishiguro's characters, this is particularly so.

It is ironic that being butchered in an operating theatre is termed "completing"; this word is as euphemistic as the gleaming white "recovery centre" in Dover where Ruth dies and where Kathy wouldn't mind ending her life- a sanitised and cleaned up representation of something very savage and pitiless.

The film adaptation – and a caution

Ishiguro was an executive producer for the film adaptation of the novel in 2010, directed by Mark Romanek. No film can include everything from a novel of any length, so artistic decisions are made about what to leave out, and where to lay the emotional emphasis.

The film plays down many of the childhood reminiscences in the novel. It is Ruth, not Madame, who sees Kathy singing to her tape; the tape does not go missing; the scientific and educational context is different. There are no male guardians in the film. The function and ethos of Hailsham is closer to an old-fashioned boarding school than to the more liberal place it is in the novel, where its main purpose is not to educate the "students" in the normal way, but to prepare them for their fate without telling them more about that than they can bear at a young age. The characterisation of Miss Lucy is very different from her character in the novel.

In the film, even at Hailsham, the emphasis is on the compatibility of Kathy and Tommy, and Ruth takes Tommy away from Kathy; they have no break-up at school, as they do in the novel. The attraction of finding your "possible" is strong; the discovery that deferral is merely a myth, and is impossible, has considerable emotional force; and the boat scene, orchestrated by Ruth so that she can seek Kathy's forgiveness, and set Tommy free to have with her the relationship he should always have had, is poignant, because it comes too late. It is a life-affirming opportunity missed, because it arrives in the shadow of death.

The film is interesting because it supports Ishiguro's comments about his own view of where the core of the book is located, in the relationships and friendships, and in the notion of making our personal peace as death becomes imminent.

By all means watch the film, if you have the chance……..but do not treat it as the basis for a critical reading of the novel. If you do see it, ask yourself whether it affects your perception of the characters at all. But you should not use it as a substitute for attentive reading of Ishiguro's writing in the novel as a whole. Because a film version can only offer edited highlights, it is incomplete. To use another analogy, the film is like "unzipping" yourself and putting some of your organs on the table. It does not reflect the true overall experience of living with the written text, because it cannot hope or aim to achieve that.

Rebellion and conforming

The novel is not interested in righteous protests, or outraged by the cruelty of the science and the society which treats these characters so badly. Ishiguro has pointed out that few people are revolutionaries; we tend to live small lives, in which we grapple with our own private difficulties. We accept those struggles and we are too preoccupied with them to protest loudly about them.

The novel's originality lies in its unsettling and provocative fusion of an Eastern acceptance of human fate (which is largely philosophical) with a characteristically English acceptance of death as something inevitable, which needs to be bowed to, politely and with good manners; we have an ingrained class system, from the feudalism of the Middle Ages onwards, which depends on the idea that we all have a more or less fixed place in society, and our role is to accept it, not protest about it.

The world in which this book is set has no difficulty in accepting that for some people to live unnaturally long lives, others must live very short ones.

While the characters in the novel simply accept the cruelty which is done to them, because , for them, it is normal, and they see no alternative (rather like being a prisoner of war in a concentration camp), the reader is less inclined to accept the world of the book so stoically.

There is some common ground between "Never Let Me Go" and George Orwell's novella "Animal Farm" (1945). While Orwell's fable is an allegory about the Russian Revolution, and about the pattern of revolution generally, it is underpinned by questions about the obligations of the individual to society, and of society to the individual; specifically, to what the English philosopher Thomas Hobbes had called "the social contract".

Hobbes (1588-1679) lived through the turmoil of the English Civil Wars, and the execution of the King, Charles 1. He argued that states and countries need to be ruled effectively by a single head of state, and that, as citizens, we enter into a "social contract"- we give up some of our personal freedoms in exchange for a guarantee that the person who runs our country will have our physical safety as their prime concern.

Hobbes' view is that when this strong contractual relationship- the obligation of governors to secure the physical safety of their subjects- breaks down, our lives become chaotic and violent.

This is the "summum malum" or the greatest evil which can befall us- our lives are then dominated by "continual fear and danger of violent death, and the life of man (is) solitary, poor, nasty, brutish and short". This robs us of the capacity to do anything productive in our lives. It is precisely the philosophy which has led Miss Emily to run Hailsham in the way she does.

I cannot think of a better way to describe the predicament Kathy and her contemporaries face. As an experienced carer, she is socially isolated or **solitary**. We learn, in Chapter 14, that social visits to carers are not permitted. In that chapter, she tells us that she likes visiting cheap department stores, where "you can hang around and enjoy yourself".

She appears to be entitled to a bedsit and a car for her work, but no salary or luxuries; she is **poor**. At the age of 31, she has perhaps two or three years of her **short** life left. She faces the prospect of a **brutish** and violent death in the operating theatre, at the time of her third or fourth donation, or, as she explains in Chapter 23, the possibility of something even worse:

"how maybe, after the fourth donation , even if you've technically completed, you're still conscious in some sort of way…….. It's horror movie stuff……"

The novel is set in England, in the late 1990s- supposedly a time of government by liberal democracy, where human rights are respected- unless you are a clone.

Viscount Hailsham was a prominent politician in Britain from the 1960s to the 1980s. It may not be entirely a coincidence that the school in the novel shares his name. He made a famous remark, when giving the Richard Dimbleby lecture in 1976, that we live "under an elective dictatorship".

By this, he meant that, once we have elected a government with a majority at a General Election, it can pass whatever laws it wants, however extreme those laws may be. The danger of this is that governments will start to neglect the rights and interests of some groups of citizens, and will be free to pursue an ideological agenda, because nobody can challenge them.

The climate of repression in Ishiguro's novel is just as authoritarian and threatening as the pigs' control of Animal Farm in Orwell's novella. Writers are often interested in the plight of the most powerless members of society, and Kathy and Tommy are certainly in that group.

Ishiguro presents us with a cold, damp, grey, but largely recognisable version of England, with its counties, its fields and its coastal towns. But he makes a simple change to the real history of science, making cancer and other terminal illnesses curable from the 1950s- but only by destroying clones which have almost all the characteristics of "normal" human beings. This is not so far removed from two issues which are close to readers' experience- the question of animal welfare (do we treat farm animals properly?) and the regulations which should apply to the donation of human organs.

When the scandal of the retention of organs for human transplant at Alder Hey Hospital and other hospitals between 1988 and 1995 came to light, a public enquiry led to the Human Tissue Act of 2004. Ishiguro's world has no such protection for any clone.

Structure and narrative organisation, and technique

The structure of the novel is worth bearing in mind. It consists of 23 chapters, in three separate sections.

Part 1 (chapters 1-9) deals with the Hailsham years, and it takes up 39% of the novel. Part 2 (chapters 10-17) covers the next phase, life at the Cottages, and it ends with Kathy's decision to start her time as a carer. It occupies 32% of the length of the novel. Part 3 (chapters 18-23) takes up the last 29% ; resolves the characters' and the reader's unanswered questions about the world of the novel; includes the deaths of Ruth and Tommy; and leaves Kathy very much on her own, with nothing ahead of her except her own "donations", disability and death.

This sounds quite straightforward, but Ishiguro creates **sustained suspense** by **delaying the explanations** of what the reader perceives as abnormal- the perversion of the meaning of the word "donation", the use of "completing" as a euphemism for death, the role of "guardians", the concepts of "deferrals" and "possibles", the impossibility of the main characters having children, the precise role of "carers", and the real function of Hailsham. In a less specific way, how the characters spend their time, what they are interested in, what they are at liberty to do and not to do, their attitudes towards shopping and sex are all points of difference between them and us. Their lives are **like ours** and **unlike ours**. Just as Miss Lucy knows that they have not been told the whole truth (because Miss Emily wants their young lives to be bearable), Ishiguro **holds back the disclosure** of the true nature of the world he has created - and, particularly, the unreality of deferrals- until the reader is ready to bear it, almost at the end of the novel.

Another important **aspect of unreality** is this; we are used to reading novels where the plot moves forward in a straight line, and events succeed each other. In "Never Let Me Go", there are really only three such episodes- the trip to Norfolk, the excursion to see the stranded boat, and the trip to Littlehampton. Otherwise, Kathy's discursive account **jumps backwards and forwards** in time, in a way which makes sense to her, but which adds to the puzzle and the suspense for the reader. Perhaps we feel that the process of reading the novel, which requires us to **thread together apparently disconnected fragments** in different parts of the narrative, gives us a little of the sense of **exhaustion** which afflicts all carers, and must affect Kathy, because she has been a carer for so long.

Among the important decisions the novelist has to make, the most obvious is whether to write in the third person or the first person. Ishiguro has Kathy narrate the novel, so that we see her world from her (limited) point of view; what puzzles her puzzles us. We find the answers at the time when she chooses to reveal them, in her narrative. This is another technical trick which maintains the reader's experience of uncertainty and suspense. Kathy addresses the person she is speaking to (who seems to be another clone, but who did not attend Hailsham), and she naturally does not need to explain **the terminology of donation** to that person. Readers, who are not clones, but are, in the terminology of the novel, "normals", are left to work out the real, precise meanings for themselves.

The novel is presented to us as **a spoken, not a written, narrative**. Why Kathy is telling her story to someone else, an unnamed person, is not explained. Is it a coincidence that the stories Kathy reads to Tommy in Chapter 20- "The Odyssey" and "One Thousand and One Nights"- come to us from an oral, not a written literary heritage? Once Kathy has gone, there will be virtually no students left with memories of Hailsham to record.

Kathy's text, or the transcript of it which we read, is certainly full of the colloquialisms and repetitions of spoken language; this does not, however, obscure the clever management of the pace of the narrative. Kathy is careful to pay close attention to her readings of others' thoughts and feelings, their looks, their possible motivations.

It is, in fact, inconceivable- in the literal sense- that anyone could recall so many episodes from their earlier life with so much precision, and particularly all the dialogue which we are expected to take as a true record of what was said. This is not to say that Kathy is not to be relied upon, as a narrator- she gives an honest account, drawn from a well-trained memory, and her judgments are often more generous to other people than they are to herself. But how many conversations you had as an eight or twelve year old can you remember every word of? And even then your childhood is fifteen years closer to you now than Kathy's is to her memory of hers.

Kathy is presented as a woman of 31. Although she has been denied the opportunity to live a fully developed life, it is arguable that the range of language she uses is less complex than her knowledge (of English Literature) and her biological age implies.

There is a directness and simplicity in the language of the novel which makes the emotional shocks and pathos or sadness it delivers more powerful than it would otherwise be.

For someone who has studied the Victorian novel, Kathy's vocabulary is still child-like. Having no parents, and very limited contact with people older than herself (apart from the guardians, who are supervisors, not developers of children), she has never had the opportunity to develop a mature language of her own. This is especially clear in the language she uses throughout the novel in relation to sex. I suggest you spend some time looking at the linguistic expressions she uses when she talks about sex, and then ask yourself how that affects your attitude towards her. Do you feel sorry for her? Frustrated by her? Sympathetic? Or, if you feel all of that, how are they combined, and what is the overall effect?

The Big Brother "society"

More broadly, Kathy and her fellow students at Hailsham are sheltered, as children and adolescents, from the awful truth that they exist to be harvested for their organs. They show no self-pity, even as the truth dawns on them; this makes us, as readers, progressively more sorry for them, and angry on their behalf.

Ishiguro presents the authoritarian morality in which these pseudo- human beings are regarded as sub-human (because they are clones) as an accepted and uncontested fact. There is none of the resistance or rebellion we find in Orwell's "Animal Farm" or "1984". No-one tries to escape, and we do not know what would be done to them if they did- it is left to our imagination (although Miss Lucy's "ghostly expression" as she talks about "terrible accidents" with electrified fences in Chapter 7 may be a clue). All we know is that the authorities send letters setting the date of each of the four successive donations (if, unlike Ruth and Chrissie, you survive the second donation); they know where you are, and the constant medical tests on donors exist in order to monitor when they will be medically fit to lose the next part of themselves.

In a sense, our battery chickens and farm animals are treated more humanely, because they do not know they are living under an extended death sentence. A single paragraph in chapter 23 confronts us with the terrible prospect that, if the fourth "donation" does not kill you, "it's horror movie stuff", with "plenty more donations", until "they switch you off". "Completion" is not always extinction; it may be, in a minority of cases, less than what we mean by death- and, somehow, much worse.

In the real world, when people are faced with this kind of oppression, they will rebel if they can. The fact that this cannot happen in the world of the novel puts the treatment of the young clones on a par with the Holocaust, but the ideology of the novel is purely scientific, not racist. However, the end result- treating the weak and helpless as subhuman- is the same.

The powerlessness - and the disinclination - of Kathy and her friends to try to escape their fate gives the novel its elegiac sense of hopelessness. She and Tommy accept the news that deferrals do not exist politely and submissively. This is an unconventional, or even an unrealistic, way to write a novel. Tommy even takes pride in his performance as a donor.

Some theorists and critics believe that all novels conform to one of seven basic story types- Overcoming the Monster, Rags to Riches, the Quest,

Voyage and Return, Rebirth, Comedy, and Tragedy (The Seven Basic Plots: Why We Tell Stories, by Christopher Booker, published by Continuum, 2005). Implicit in each of these story templates (even perhaps in tragedy) is a process of growing up, AND a sense that the world has undergone some kind of restoration or rebirth by the time the tale ends.

"Animal Farm" is an exception to this principle, because it ends with the pigs in a position of complete control and authority; "Never Let Me Go" is similar, because it crushes Kathy's (and our) hope of a "deferral" by revealing, without compassion, the awful truth- that Hailsham was merely a less inhumane oasis in a wider desert of cruelty. This offends our natural desire for a happy ending, in order to reinforce the argument that authoritarianism, once indulged, is like a small fire with a supply of oxygen- it grows, and becomes almost impossible to put out.

Ishiguro is not interested in science in itself, but he is concerned, as many contemporary writers are, about the dilemmas which the demands of developed societies for advances in science create. In order to satisfy its (or our) appetite for progress, for curing the previously incurable, and for "medical advances", animals and human beings have to be experimented on.

The science of cloning and stem cell research has made the possibility of replacing defective genes very real. Ethical questions arise, about disability, the end of life, and genetic selection. If genetic selection is in the hands of the wrong people, it can be used to create a master race- a political or racist application- rather than to eliminate disease. The cultural resistance to genetically modified crops illustrates the unscientific public's scepticism about the application of scientific discovery. As Ishiguro shows us, this ceases to apply where issues of life or death arise; if we can use science to keep ourselves alive, we tend to forget the ethical questions. In the novel, once clone technology becomes a threat- because it can engineer genetically enhanced humans- the welfare of clones becomes a taboo subject. Why would we give a good life to a "creature" which has the potential to take our place in the genetic hierarchy, and which threatens our control of it?

Ishiguro is not interested in being too precise about the scientific basis for the novel. The science which haunts the reader is to do with which organs we can live without. What "donations" can we survive? The list is a long one- kidney, pancreas, liver, eyes, lung, stomach, intestine, sex organs- anything except, in the end, the brain and the heart. And, in the end, even they may not be safe.

In Chapter 22, Miss Emily lists the diseases the clones exist to cure- cancer, motor neurone disease, heart disease. It follows that the clones will be required to supply any organ which can be transplanted into people who suffer from any of these conditions.

The novel manages to convey the pain for the donor which is the legacy of these disfigurements, not just for Tommy, with his bleeding and his kidney trouble, but, quite graphically, in the description of Ruth's death at the end of Chapter 19. It leaves the clones longing for "completion"- death- as they face their fourth donation.

Although Kazuo Ishiguro says that he did not want to excite a sense of outrage in his reader, we cannot escape the sense that a so-called society which leaves its most vulnerable members longing to die is not really a society at all. It is certainly not civilised.

Commentary and analysis

Closed-book exams, where you cannot refer to a copy of the novel, make it especially important that you know the plot and the key moments in the narrative. Your exam also requires you to analyse the content of the text for meaning.

So the next part of this guide gives you a chapter by chapter analysis and commentary. You should read a chapter, then read the commentary here, and see what you agree or disagree with, and what observations of your own you want to add.

Chapter 1

The opening chapter introduces us to Kathy, and to Ruth and Tommy. **None of them is immediately a sympathetic character**; Tommy, at the age of twelve, is prone to toddler-like outbursts, and Kathy and Ruth both exhibit a strong lack of empathy, a degree of emotional detachment, in their dealings with others. It is only as we become more familiar with their circumstances that we see that these are **not normal children, and so they cannot be judged by normal criteria**.

Kathy's narrative monologue plunges us into her world, a world she supposes we are familiar with. The addressee, she says, may be a "carer", just as she is- the assumption is that the reader already knows and understands Kathy's world, although we do not. There are **elements of this world** which **seem normal**- school, hospital, having a profession- **but in each case there is something strange and unfamiliar undermining that apparent normality.**

Kathy is often harsh; she tells the donors she cares for "to snap out of it", and she seems to be unsentimental. She takes pride in her results. Being good at her job "means a lot" to her. She thinks that other people envy her for **her bedsit and her car**- things we think of as just normal, not a cause of envy. She is looking forward to **"finishing at last"** after twelve years of being a carer- **an odd way of regarding a job you take pride in** (she will describe

28

the emotional exhaustion her job generates at the start of Chapter 18).

Where she lives, and **what she will do next**, are **not disclosed**. There is **no mention of a family or close relationships**. She drives "all over the country", which seems "empty" and underpopulated. Because she is not as compassionate as we would expect a nurse to be, we cannot be sure whether Kathy's feeling that she is resented by some of her colleagues is justified or not.

She is **not a nurse in the sense we are familiar with**; she does not work in a single location, and for the last six years she has been able to choose her patients.

This chapter introduces the important concept of donors and donating. **We think of donating as voluntary**. We donate goods to charity shops; we give blood donations; we may carry a donor card, which allows our organs to be used for transplants in the event of our own death. There are **hints that the donations in the novel are different, and in fact not posthumous but life-threatening**; donors can become "agitated", even before the "fourth donation", and some donors do not survive for long after their third donation. But there is **no indication- at this stage- that these "donations" are compulsory** - because both carers and donors take it as read that the system and rules of donation are simply accepted. So do Kathy and the person to whom she is telling her story.

Just as **a "recovery centre" is not quite, or really, a hospital**, **Hailsham is not quite, or really, a school**. It has "guardians" instead of teachers, and it is a privileged estate, a place you are lucky to be at, where children grow up together. It is not so much a boarding school as an all-inclusive, more comfortable children's residential home or hotel, but with some important, though unmentioned, differences- there are **no holidays, no parental visits, no family homes to go to, no excursions.**

The ill-fated, unnamed donor Kathy had looked after nine years ago had wanted to assimilate, as his own, her memories of Hailsham, because to remember his own growing up in Dorset merely elicited a "new kind of grimace"- it had nothing but its own pain. In chapter 22, Miss Emily will explain that Hailsham hid the fact that all the children there would be killed for their organs. In Dorset and elsewhere, there was no such care or protection. The closure of Hailsham makes that harsh cruelty inescapable for all clone children, however young they are.

There is **a single use in chapter 1 of the term "completing"- a euphemism for "dying".**

Death is a taboo term in this novel, and it is used only very occasionally (for example, in chapter 5, referring to the ghost of the girl who went outside Hailsham to explore, and in Chapter 9, describing the "dead hour" after lessons are finished- or "completed"?- for the day).

The action in this opening chapter is largely in the past- Ruth is in the past, the unnamed donor is in the past, and Hailsham is in the past. Hailsham, though, still exerts an influence on Kathy in the present- she looks for it, as though it has been transplanted into a new location. **The idea of Hailsham is "lucky" and consoling.** The truth about Hailsham emerges in Chapter 18- it has been sold to a hotel chain.

It is troubling that a young woman aged 31 thinks in terms of the past so much- as if her life is already over. We do not understand at this point that the switch from carer to donor is effectively the decisive step towards an extended dying.

We are not sure what has happened to Tommy. There is no explicit indication at this stage that he, too, has "completed". More than half the chapter is devoted to the incident in which Tommy, the best footballer in the group, is humiliated by not being chosen for either team. His reaction- a furious raving, screaming, shouting and swearing (at no-one in particular) is **an outburst at the injustice** of it. It **foreshadows what Tommy does in chapter 22**.

The interest here is not so much in the incident of the football match as in the reaction to it of Kathy, Ruth and the other girls. The girls who watch the event say that **Tommy is picked on because he is "a layabout" who does not try to be creative; Ruth calls him a "mad animal". He refuses to conform and to accept** what the other boys inflict on him, and his **rebellion is judged as uncivilised and immature**.

This lack of empathy and compassion is a defensive mechanism, because the girls feel guilty about watching someone else having distress forced on him; or perhaps they recognise (subconsciously) that Tommy's rebellion is in some sense comical, but, in a deeper sense, right, however futile it is. Kathy and Tommy discuss this again in the final two paragraphs of chapter 22; they tend to agree there that Tommy did indeed have some special insight into the soulless unfairness of his, and their, situation.

Authoritarian societies depend on the concept that rebelling, or refusing to conform, is socially unacceptable, and deserves to be punished.

Kathy's account has her going to Tommy, apart from the other girls. She expresses concern about his polo shirt, but she is really showing **a disguised concern for him**. Tommy's rage subsides after Kathy touches him on his arm. This is an arresting gesture because the children are unused to any form of touch, concern or emotional intimacy.

The dead donor had asked Kathy which guardian was her "special favourite". The residents of Hailsham carry childish ideas about attachment, love, sex and intimacy into their "adult" lives because they are banned from having children of their own, and they have no role models for romantic relationships.

The idea that we feel guilty seeing others suffer, by being voyeuristic ("taking out ringside seats"), helps to contextualise **Hailsham; these children have been separated from the rest of the world, so that they are out of sight and out of mind.** A blind eye can be turned to their welfare and their cruel fate- although they are the lucky and privileged few.

Kathy's narrative goes further to legitimise the children's being victimised.

She explains that, given the freedom to select her own donors to care for, she gravitates towards those who were at Hailsham (though few survive now), because they are somehow easier to care for. She justifies this as "natural"- **"you choose your own kind".**

This is a cultural and anthropological justification for the cloning of human organs- who would choose a pig's organs when they can have a human's?

It also helps to create a perspective in which Kathy and her colleagues never seek help from the "possibles" or others in the external world which treats them as sub-human.

Their former guardians are the only people they can go to; their status as an underclass, pariahs (like the caste system in India) condemns them to an unrealised life and an early death.

Chapter 2

This chapter extends the topic of Tommy's struggle for acceptability, and how it was resolved.

There is an important hint that Kathy will also have to "donate" and "complete"- she tells us that **she "wouldn't mind at all" if she "ended up" at Ruth's "recovery centre" in Dover**. She addresses the reader as someone who faces the same fate, but did not attend Hailsham.

The medicals "almost every week" are too intense to be the routine of a school. The sense that there is more to them than meets the eye is intensified in Chapter 6, where Miss Lucy's emphasis on the absolute necessity for the children of keeping healthy and not smoking is dressed up as a consequence of them being **"special"**. This is **ironic**; not smoking is not for their benefit, but for the benefit of the recipients of their organs.

The seasonal Exchanges- a type of flea market or car boot sale- are another foreign element to any definition of Hailsham as a school. **The children have no money**, but they use "exchange tokens"- **a more primitive and less evolved method of payment**- to buy the creative work of others in their year- this is the only way of acquiring personal possessions. These aspects of Hailsham are more like an Army barracks; you could see them as a way of reinforcing the identity of **a group culture or "esprit de corps" which regimentalises the thinking of everyone**

concerned. The reason soldiers train and live so closely together is that it is a guarantee that they will do what is expected of them later, even if that means certain death.

Later, we will discover that **the emphasis on creativity** is the initiative of Madame and Miss Emily- the head guardian- who are fighting a secret battle **to prove to the utilitarian scientists and politicians that the clone children have a soul, an identity, and are fully human**. For now, though, we see the issue of "creating" from a child's point of view- "how you were regarded......liked....respected....had to do with how good you were at creating". Accepting and conforming to the way you are expected to behave protects you. Miss Geraldine, who is the soul of kindness, praises Tommy's childish drawing of an elephant in tall grass, instead of ridiculing it. The Senior 2 boys then persecute Tommy, with a fairly predictable range of practical jokes and exclusion techniques.

Tommy is accepted again once he has controlled his responses. He has found an inner calm after **Miss Lucy tells him that there is no compulsion to be creative**; she knows that it is of no importance in the longer term. In chapter 7, three years later, **when the children are aged 16, Miss Lucy tells them the truth- that they will not have jobs or careers, because they will soon be starting to donate their vital organs, and will not live into middle age.** In chapter 9, she tries to retract what she has told

Tommy here ("the other guardians had been right all along") and that chapter ends with the departure of Miss Lucy, because she was indiscreet enough to tell the children the truth about their futures.

Chapter 2 repeats and reinforces material in chapter 1. In both chapters, we read about Tommy's exclusions by other boys. In both, Ruth says he deserves what he gets; the girls, as a group, respond with detachment; we read about Tommy's tantrums, his refusal to be creative and his failure to contribute to the Spring Exchange; we see **Kathy trying to help and encourage him to be less of a victim.** In both chapters, someone mimics Tommy- Laura in chapter 1, whom the other girls, apart from Kathy, encourage; and Arthur H in chapter 2, whom the boys ignore.

In chapter 1, **Kathy's thoughts in the present** (that she will stop being a carer soon and become a donor; and that wherever she goes she is looking for Hailsham) **are interrupted by episodes from the past**- the donor who was dying nine years ago, and the football episode when she and Tommy were aged 12. Again, chapter 2 is similar. It opens with more about that year (Senior 2); then Kathy recalls her conversation in Dover with Ruth (probably about seven years earlier), after Ruth's first donation; she recalls Tommy's own account of the bullying, which they had discussed - this leads to another extended episode from that time at Hailsham.

Kathy naturally thinks that Tommy is lying about the guardian's emphasis on the unimportance of creativity. It is important that we see her struggling with this radical idea, and being reluctant to accept it; and that her relationship with Tommy should be difficult. Even in a deeply conformist setting, the novelist must create dramatic tension if the reader's interest is to be maintained.

Tommy and Kathy share a hunger for fairness, and they have an instinct to be compassionate. But they will find that there are no deferrals, no exceptions, and that, although aspects of life at Hailsham can be uncomfortable, it is preferable to what comes afterwards. In the final chapter, Tommy says that he and Kathy have always shared a drive to "find things out"- to know the truth.

Chapter 3

The final two paragraphs of this chapter take us into darker territory; we will examine them more closely in a few minutes' reading time.

This chapter consists of an extension of the conversation Kathy and Tommy had started in the lunch queue. It becomes more far-ranging, **provoking us to think about the relationship between the children and the guardians, and the ways in which they are not the same as teachers.**

The children begin to examine possible motives for the apparently strange behaviour of Miss Lucy and Madame. Miss Lucy will speak for herself soon enough, in the remainder of part 1. We will have to **wait until almost the end of the novel for Madame to explain herself**.

We begin, here, to sense that cruelty (to an innocent underclass) cannot exist without some degree of compassion. Guardians cannot be completely dispassionate about what happens to children in their care day by day, even though their fate is unavoidable. This forms an interesting contrast with Kathy's observations at the start of the novel- "carers" can quite easily become exhausted, as donors on the verge of "completing" can be "agitated".

Tommy wants to tell Kathy all of what Miss Lucy had said to him; Kathy teases him, by accident, and feels sorry. Miss Lucy had asked Tommy to tell her how he had come to be treated so badly, but, before long, "she'd broken in"; she is outraged that Tommy should be criticised or punished because he is not as creative as others, and, especially, that the misplaced stress on creativity evades the more important question of **what is being taught and why** ("she'd a good mind to talk to us about it herself"); and, when she does, she is removed from any influence over the children, suddenly and decisively, at the end of chapter 9.

I have read that in some parts of the world convicted criminals can be freed but at any time, without notice, they can be required to step inside a coach which is really a death chamber- without warning, they are put to death and their organs are harvested. Is this more humane than what Miss Lucy wants- a full disclosure of what the future threatens? And, if it is, **how old do we need to be before we should be given this information about the timing and nature of our own death?**

Because they know what will be done to the children, the guardians find it difficult to reprimand them; discipline seems to be slacker than in many schools. Mr Frank "was trying to teach us spelling"- presumably, without much success; eleven-year-olds, in Mr Roger's class, would "laugh and laugh". Miss Geraldine is comforting; Miss Lucy does not referee the boys' football matches- she joins in. So, although Tommy has had "lecture(s)" from several guardians, "including Miss Emily herself", **Hailsham is as relaxed as they can make it**- in chapter 1, the Juniors were able to ask to have their **lesson in the pavilion**!

Miss Lucy will sometimes acknowledge Tommy with "a little nod" because, knowing how his life will end, she will not accept that he should be criticised, falsely, for a lack of effort. Perhaps because she can see how resilient he has been, she (like Miss Geraldine) looks for things in him to praise, and tells him that he is "a very good student". Whether this comment strays beyond what is judged proper in a guardian-child relationship is not commented on. **Recognising the worth and individuality of the condemned is a**

dangerous habit to develop because it could turn to pity and sympathy, and then to rebellion.

Kathy tells us (rather than showing us) that, in the past, Miss Lucy's responses had consistently been unexpected or unconventional. In chapter 22, Miss Emily says that "if she'd had her way, your happiness at Hailsham would have been shattered".

The acceptance Tommy wins from Miss Lucy is different from the experience all the children have of **Madame. With her short hair, her sharp suit, her chilly look and her distant manner, she keeps her visits as brief as possible**, although she has been coming to Hailsham ever since it opened (because she is its principal, and the champion, with Miss Emily, of the humane treatment of cloned children).

As an eight year old, Ruth had hit on the truth- that **Madame was afraid of the children**. The amateurish, childish plan to "swarm out" around her does provide the scientific proof of Ruth's theory. Madame **shudders with revulsion**, and she cannot bear the thought that one of the children might brush against her by accident; she has a physical aversion to them, as if she is afraid of spiders and they are the spiders (to put it like an eight year old). The group of six girls cannot understand how Madame's dread of them can be consistent with her taking their best art for "her gallery"- a question Kathy is still asking, with Tommy, in the earlier part of this chapter, at the age of thirteen- five years on. The shudders, the revulsion, the

Gallery, and the talk of spiders are crucial in Chapter 22- they refer back to this chapter.

In the closing paragraphs of the chapter, Kathy- as the narrator of the novel- relates the experience of the eight year olds to that of her addressee (who has had guardians), and to the reader (who has not). She observes that this was, for them, the moment when **they realised** they were separate or **different from both their guardians and from the rest of the world- an ethnic or biological minority**. Because the gardeners and the delivery men would "joke and laugh", the force of the serious information-"all the talks, videos, discussions, warnings"- was diluted. Madame's physical reaction to the mere possibility of physical contact with a clone cannot be ignored; it tells you that you are **revolting, rejected, cast out, and not valued or loved.**

The realisation that you are "different" is made worse by the fact that Madame and anyone like her "shudder" even though they do not hate you or wish you harm. They cannot see you as an individual; **all they can see is "how you were brought into this world and why"**. To realise the strength of their rejection of you, and the reasons for it, is "a cold moment". Kathy says that, even at the age of eight, they have been living for a couple of years with an inner voice which is predicting just this experience of being frozen out.

Chapter 4

The main purpose of this chapter is to develop **the characterisation of Miss Emily**, the head of Hailsham, and to prepare for the plot development which Kathy outlines in the opening paragraph- the children's curiosity about Madame "kept growing….. to dominate our lives".

Miss Emily is described in detail. Although she is softly spoken, she is **intimidating, yet reassuring.** She does not shout or rant, and she often seems to be distracted or abstracted. The children cannot understand her long homilies in assemblies after bad behaviour at the Sales, but Kathy remembers the key phrases "misuse of opportunity" and **"unworthy of privilege"**. There is a degree of irony here, because these phrases belong to the world of the private school. Hailsham students are privileged in the sense that they are treated more humanely than others, but it is **a limited privilege**, because they have no real opportunity- no chance of escaping being killed before they are middle-aged. The critics of Hailsham would argue that these children are indeed unworthy of privilege.

She is experiencing **a conflict between the need to appear authoritarian and her natural sympathy for the children.** In chapter 22, she will tell Tommy that the Gallery was intended to prove that the clone children "had souls". Her belief was that "students……reared in humane environments….grow to be as sensitive as any human". In the late 1970s the moral argument, that the forced donors were in fact "fully human", was gathering force. This coincides with the period Kathy concentrates on- from the age of 10 to 13- which we can place as approximately 1977 to 1980.

The argument here- that creatures bred to be killed for the use of humans have rights, and deserve to be treated properly, with regard to their general welfare- reminds us of the ongoing debate about animal rights. The idea that you can treat **children as animals you will slaughter** (and eat!!) had been taken further by **the satirist Jonathan Swift**, in his famous essay from 1729, "A modest proposal for preventing the children of Ireland from being a burden to their parents or country". Tongue-in-cheek, he argues (in a deliberately outrageous way) that the solution to a rising birth rate in poor families is to sell their children for food, like farm animals.

The references to the assorted junk which is brought in for the Sales as a "bumper crop" are unsettling, because of its agricultural and harvesting connotations. We can imagine a hospital somewhere receiving a delivery of harvested clone organs and asking the same grotesque question.

When Kathy sees **Miss Emily** "wandering around, talking to herself", and when, in Senior 3 (aged 13) she sees her practising a speech to an invisible audience, she is rehearsing what she will say at conferences attended by "all sorts of famous people". She **is frustrated when the children occasionally behave badly, because this weakens her argument.** Hence the question she asks herself out loud- "What thwarts us?". She is always preoccupied with the question of how she can improve the welfare and perception of her students and her humane education system.

When the children were 10, Miss Lucy would not explain the real purpose of the gallery, because she felt the children were too young to deal with the implications of the extent to which the outside world viewed them as of only scientific value.

The "tokens controversy" is further evidence that **the guardians want to support the children's emotional development.** The sales are usually disappointing, but, even so, the children cannot shake off their feelings of "hope and excitement".

The guardians want to make the children's lives as normal as possible for as long as possible, while Miss Emily is also fighting an external campaign to alter the fundamental principles of the "donations programme". Kathy and her friends and classmates **repeatedly find that the guardians are more sympathetic and gentle with them than they expect.**

The remainder of the chapter deals with Kathy's early dealings with Ruth, between the ages of 5 and 8; it highlights **Ruth's** imagination, her **tendency to**

become irritated without notice or explanation, and the power of her disapproval, as Kathy felt it. However, Ruth must approve of Kathy, because she admits her to the select group of Miss Geraldine's "secret guards".

Chapter 5

Just as Kathy and Tommy disagree on when the tokens controversy took place, Kathy and Ruth have different recollections of how long the secret guarding of Miss Geraldine continued for. Here, Kathy describes it as an extended episode, ending when Ruth excluded her from the group after Kathy was (naturally) disappointed to find that Ruth did not actually know the rules of chess.

Ruth had bluffed over her chess-playing expertise, and she **bluffs** over the plot to abduct Miss Geraldine, and also over the origin of the pencil case (three years later) which she bought in a Sale. Later in the narrative, Ruth bluffs over the rumours that Hailsham students can secure deferrals, and she bluffs over the normality of Kathy's sexual feelings and about her own fidelity to Tommy.

Building on Ruth's imaginary horses, there is a degree of fantasising in her temperament. All children have an imaginative "reality" as well as the reality of the lives they live; at the age of 8 or 9, when Moira observes that the Miss Geraldine plot is infantile, Kathy finds herself angry, because she is not ready to reduce the role of imagination, and enlarge the role of reality- "Moira was suggesting she and I cross some line …… I didn't want that….. for any of us".

The power and strength of **Ruth**'s imagination has brought her a position of leadership and power among her friends. She **seeks to reinforce her aura of superiority with the (risky) lie** that the pencil case is a gift from Miss Geraldine, an outrageous, rule-breaking favour. Kathy exposes the lie, and confronts Ruth with it. In doing so, she shocks herself with her own capacity to distress and upset her best friend. But the lies Ruth confesses to in Chapter 19 do far more harm to her relationship with Kathy.

Three years earlier, **Kathy's loyalty to Ruth** had remained intact, even after Ruth excluded her. The fierceness with which she dismisses Moira demonstrates that.

The idea that a group of 8 year olds can protect Miss Geraldine from a dangerous abduction is absurd; it is also **an inversion of the guardian-child relationship**. If there really were a plot to kidnap Miss Geraldine and take her to the woods in a van, the children would be unable to prevent it; just as **the guardians are, in truth, unable to keep the children from being taken** – symbolically- to "something harder and darker" in **the woods**- a place children haunt, and **where children have been maimed, disfigured and murdered, which is precisely the fate of a clone.**

All the eight and nine year olds can do is to gather "more and more evidence" of the non-existent plot. The children are completely powerless; and although the plot against Miss Geraldine is just imagined, the danger to them , when they are really taken to **the "woods", the real, dark, fatal world beyond Hailsham House**, will be only too real.

The plot to abduct Miss Geraldine is just a myth, in the same way that the rumour of a deferral, or of special privileges beyond Hailsham for Hailsham students, is a myth. The latter part of the novel replaces myths with hard truths about how and when various childhood friends of Kathy's have died. Eventually, she is just about the only one left.

The desire of the child to protect the guardian is "pathetic" in the sense of the Greek term pathos- it inspires sympathy in us, while we recognise how futile it is. The degree of pathos we feel, as readers, is intensified because we know what these children do not; they have not grasped the perils ahead, because Miss Lucy and the other guardians will not tell them the horrific truth until they are about to leave, at the age of 16.

The chapter dwells on the woods, and their power to terrify the young. They loom over the house, and cast a shadow which is as much emotional as literal. The emotional shadow is intermittent, because Kathy sometimes feels "a defiant surge of courage"; but the woods have secrets. The "terrible stories" of ghosts and murdered children, and of cruel guardians, are "nonsense", according to the present guardians, but the older children say that the younger ones will "be told the ghastly truth soon enough".

Hailsham is, here, called Hailsham House; it is less an institution, in this chapter, than **a solid bulwark against the horrors of the woods; but children cannot stay there for ever.**

Chapter 6

This chapter includes an important short episode about smoking, and the major scene with Kathy, Madame and Kathy's tape, which gives the novel its title.

Kathy feels resourceless to restore her friendship with Ruth, and only manages to because of arbitrary opportunities to side with Ruth in public. While we all know that teenage and pre-teen girls have rapidly shifting friendships, we are conscious here that these children have no-one to help them with their relationships; **the guardians do not offer support or guidance as a parent or sibling might.**

Ruth seems ashamed and crushed; Kathy is remorseful, tearful and frustrated. There is no uncomplicated happiness here; these children are having to deal with strong emotions very much on their own. **They feel embarrassed and unnerved**

when a guardian is asked an awkward question. Many topics- especially the question of their futures- are off-limits. This remains true all the way until Chapter 22.

Kathy tells us that, in a vague way, even at the age of 9 or 10, "we knew ……… **there were donations waiting for us"- a clause which suggests, ironically, that they were to be given donations, not that they will have to donate themselves.**

The smoking discussion is, in a way, an authentic record of public health education in schools in the 1970s. Secondary schools- including the one I attended- were expected to have anti-smoking lessons, and we saw pickled lungs, which I can remember, and information films, which I can't. But **the admonition that Hailsham students are "special" (because they must keep their to-be-donated organs healthy) and must not damage their physical health in any way is a perversion of the anti-smoking message, because its purpose is to protect the health of others,** and to exploit these children; it is not in any sense for their benefit.

The children do not press Miss Lucy to explain this because, subconsciously, they know that it leads them into the ghastly world of the woods, as it were; although Kathy observes that Miss Lucy would have answered fully, if they had asked- unlike the Gallery question in chapter 4, which she had refused to answer. Miss Lucy is moving towards the truth-telling which brings about her departure at the end of chapter 9.

Her answer in chapter 4 – "all I can tell you is that it's for a good reason"- is an evasion which Kathy adopts, when Marge asks about Ruth's pencil case. Children, like guardians, are learning to keep privileged information secret.

I wonder how Miss Emily's inability to provide pictures of Norfolk would be received if she were expected to teach about all the counties! **Kathy is not clear about the reasons which determine what they are being taught, but** perhaps **it does not matter if bits of England are ignored; Norfolk is, to England, like one of the vital organs which the children will have to do without. A less than whole person can get by with a less than complete education.**

Kathy's account of the disappearance of her tape leaves it open to the reader, if not to her, that Madame may have taken it because she could not bear a recurrence of what she saw Kathy do with her pillow for a baby. Kathy's fantasy, based on an eccentric reading of the song's words, is that a woman who had been told she could not have a child miraculously does. **Madame** is affected because she **knows what Kathy does not- "none of us could have babies". Just as the novel nowhere specifies what the "vital organs" are, it is not clear how this ban on reproduction is enforced; it is all the darker and more menacing for that.**

Kathy had kept her tape secret because of the smoking image on the cover. She was 11, so the year is 1978, "a few years before Walkmans", which were first sold in the UK in 1980. The title and artist Ishiguro has invented has invited speculation. My own theory is that the name "Bridgewater" may be an allusion to the famous Simon and Garfunkel album "Bridge over troubled water". Why? Well, remove "bridge" and "water" and the remaining words- "over troubled"- are a simple anagram of "trouble" and "Dover".

Ruth's difficulties with Kathy come to a head in Dover; and Simon and Garfunkel had arguments and differences, which complicated their working relationship, but which they eventually overcame. As for the title of Kathy's tape, Songs After Dark- abbreviate it and what you have, as its initials, is SAD.

The extended analysis of the story she attaches to the words of the song is important, as is the fact that the song gives the novel its title. Kathy turns it into a song about attachment to your child, and motherhood- the relationship which is to be denied to the clone children. Kathy's feelings demonstrate that these children are indeed wholly human in the emotional sense. Hailsham itself is the nearest equivalent to the baby for Kathy. Miss Lucy's concern is that, in being 'told and not told', the awareness of their futures the children develop is approximate and therefore misleading.

Kathy is shocked to realise that Madame is in the corridor, observing her, and crying, with her usual expression of distaste, but, also, "something extra in that look". Kathy is "really unsettled" and senses some "deeper significance". What unsettles her is the fact that Madame gives her no directions and does not assert herself, although she is the adult; she does not explain her own distress. **The children are not aware that the guardians may feel sorry for them.** The reader's feelings are aligned with Madame's, because we know so much more about Kathy's plight than she does herself.

The explanation arrives in chapter 22, and it is worth looking at that while you also read chapter 6. Madame explains " **I saw a new world coming rapidly…. a little girl…… pleading, never to let her go**". The helplessness and vulnerability of the students causes her real grief.

Kathy and Tommy discuss this incident in 1980, when they are 12/13, by when they both understand that no clone will have a child. Tommy's explanation is a logical one, but he misses the broader dimension, that **the children are developing normal human instincts at Hailsham which will never be fulfilled or satisfied**. Their humane treatment makes them civilised, but this sophistication makes their slaughter more poignant than if they were dumb creatures, like their contemporaries elsewhere in the country.

Miss Emily defends the Hailsham project (in chapter 22) for its outcomes- " you're educated and cultured".

This turned out to be counter-productive, because society would not accept the threat posed by the Morningdale experiment, which threatened to facilitate "created children....demonstrably superior".

Madame does not admit to being responsible for the tape's disappearance, and there is no indication that she was. The quest to replace it adds momentum to part 2 of the novel, but it depends on this **unexplained loss** of the original tape.

At the age of 11, Kathy says, you would feel disloyal if you indulged private emotions. **The general lack of privacy at Hailsham- and, afterwards, at the Cottages- is designed to make it harder to find the physical space and time for reflection, analysis, deeper thought.**

Ruth's gesture, in finding a replacement/ substitute tape for Kathy, illustrates the principle that one good turn deserves another. While the children adopt this code of behaviour, the society they exist in is not so gracious. In giving life to others, they are killed.

In the last dozen lines of the chapter, Kathy observes that the tape Ruth bought for her is now "one of my most precious possessions". In **the absence of any physical intimacy**- the children have never experienced it- Kathy had "squeezed one of her hands in both mine" as an expression of joy and affection. The replacement tape Ruth gives Kathy is not the same as the original; but Kathy does unearth a copy, or clone, of her prized possession, in Norfolk, with Tommy, in Chapter 15.

Kathy will, in turn, hold Ruth's "hand in both of mine, squeezing whenever another flood of pain made her twist away", when Ruth dies at the end of Chapter 19. Ruth, like Kathy's original tape, has gone (to Norfolk?). The precise linguistic repetition describing the hand-holding reaffirms, at the very end of Ruth's life, Kathy's loyalty and appreciation.

Chapter 7

This chapter records the process by which the issue of donations became no longer ignored, no longer joked about, but "**sombre and serious**".

It includes four separate episodes; Miss Lucy's lesson about concentration camps; her subsequent truth-telling about the children's futures; Miss Emily's sex lectures; and Tommy's elbow and the concept of "unzipping".

The overall effect is that **knowing is different from not knowing**. As Miss Lucy puts it "you've been told and not told". From an early age, the children have absorbed some awareness of the idea of donations (from as young as 5, Kathy has already told us) but the personal impact and implications have never been explained. It is similar with sex, which the (sterile?) clones may be at risk of treating less seriously and respectfully than people in the wider world.

The idea that "donation" can be a painless process is a childish or naïve one, but it also creates an alternative reality, as a way of making the cruel bearable. Later, the concept of deferrals will fulfil the same need.

Is it better to know the awful truth? Miss Lucy's abrupt departure from Hailsham derives from her insistence that ignorance compromises the quality of the students' short lives- "you've got to know and know properly". There is no point in entertaining fantasies about acting or even working in a supermarket, when your future has been predetermined.

Miss Emily's (opposite) view is that ignorance is bliss; the students, sheltered and protected from knowing the truth of what lies ahead for them, can be "absorbed in ..... lessons". Knowing too much would have shattered their happiness.

A little knowledge leads to curiosity for more. Lectures about the emotional complications of sex will fan a desire to experiment, both within and after Hailsham; Miss Lucy might presumably argue that a short life may as well be a stimulated one.

For children up to the age of 13, donations are a taboo subject, too vaguely unpleasant to be discussed; then, at 13, they become the subject of jokes. Even when the students are 15, Miss Lucy's insistence that "it's not so far off" is met by "uncomfortable faces" which inhibit her from going on to spell out the details of the process of donation and what will be taken from them. Eventually, the unzipping jokes recede, and donation is not openly discussed, but it is no longer a joke. This sequence- taboo, joke, puzzlement, curiosity, information, experience - is applied to donations, but it emulates closely our own teenage experiences, in the non-fictional world, of finding out, not about donations, but about sex.

Tommy and Kathy disagree on whether the gradual dripfeeding of information into young minds, so that "nothing came as a complete surprise" when it was discussed more openly, is a deliberate and carefully timed strategy, or something more haphazard. The effect is of conditioning or brainwashing the children into accepting their fate. **Miss Lucy's** discomfort at the jokes about the grotesqueness of being held as a prisoner of war and being able to commit suicide by touching an electrified fence is interesting. Her **allusion to "terrible accidents" may imply that anyone who tries to escape is electrocuted; or that the guardians are especially concerned to keep the awareness of the possibility of suicide out of the students' minds.** The guardians' approach- but not Miss Lucy's- is designed, according to Miss Emily in chapter 22, to ensure that **"no doubts ever crossed your minds"; that a happier childhood can keep terror at bay.**

The reference to "My Fair Lady" (probably the 1964 film) is, as with all of Ishiguro's references to other texts, capable of helping us to see what the novel is driving at. In the film (based on Shaw's play "Pygmalion"), an uneducated girl is given elocution lessons, and becomes acceptable to high society. The clone children at Hailsham respond to their education by proving that they have souls and individuality; this should mean that they are no longer regarded as merely a source of human organs, but their education does not make them more acceptable to the world they exist to serve.

Chapter 8

This chapter records some of the students' growing concerns about their future. The guardians' approach to sex education leaves the students unclear about what is expected of them. Kathy feels anxious and left behind. Tommy and Ruth have a "serious bust-up", which disrupts Kathy's own careful plan to have a sex **experiment** with Harry C.

Tommy, too, is unsettled and on the verge of losing his self-control. This is partly as a consequence of a second conversation he has had with Miss Lucy, which has left him confused. When Kathy shows him Patricia C's calendar, Tommy is sensitive about his lack of art production. This will become a much more serious concern when he comes to contemplate , first,

Ruth's intention to seek a deferral, and then his trip with Kathy to try to secure it.

A few days before this event, Kathy has seen Miss Lucy in room 22, defacing pages of neat writing in a manic way. This scene is a neat reversal of Madame's seeing Kathy with her tape in chapter 6. Madame had said nothing, and neither, here, does Kathy explain how she came to be observing Miss Lucy. **Just as Madame was overcome, privately, by sadness over Kathy's future, Kathy now fears "something…..awful…. to do with Miss Lucy".**

Kathy's feelings of anger are rooted in the unspoken perception that **the guardians are no longer so effective at protecting and sheltering the students from the future beyond Hailsham**; indeed, they may feel that it is pointless to try to do so when students are in their final year. **Ishiguro has spoken in interviews about this aspect of parent-child relationships, saying that parents naturally want to make their children's early experiences of the world positive and reassuring, but that this protection has to cease eventually, so that older children find the adult world disappointing- hence the grey and blank landscape and skyscape he creates for the world outside Hailsham.**

The rules at Hailsham inhibit the opportunity for students to maintain sexual relationships, but the guardians do not discipline those who break the rules- Miss Emily makes an excuse and turns a blind eye to such activity. Books and films are not censored for their sexual content, unlike their representation of smoking.

The uncertainty which the guardians' ambivalent attitude to student sex engenders gives rise to several theories, including two ominous ideas- that, to be a "good donor" with good organs (kidneys, pancreas) you need to be sexually active, and that, being "normal", the guardians are uncomfortable with the fact that, for the students, reproductive sex is impossible. Kathy records comments by Miss Emily which, confusingly, acknowledge that sex is both a physical urge and that it should be emotionally satisfying- two criteria which are difficult to achieve at Hailsham, and, it seems, beyond it.

It is notable that **the language Kathy and the others use to describe sex is immature and functional- the absurd denoting of gay sex as "umbrella sex", and Kathy's repeated use of the matter of fact phrase "doing it", as well as "going at it, right, left and centre".**

Kathy does not see what Miss Lucy is "gouging" with pencil. She is scrubbing out neat blue handwriting with a pencil, using "furious lines". The subsequent news from Tommy- that she had retracted her advice that art and creativity were not important- suggests that she is defacing her own writing, her own thoughts and ideas about what guardians should say to students. She may now sense that the ideological need for the students to be "told" (how short and limited their lives will be) is, as Miss Emily thinks, well-meaning, "theoretical", but ill-judged, because it unsettles the children.

The central theme in this chapter is Ishiguro's question about protecting or sheltering children; is 16 a suitable age at which to indulge experimental behaviour? What kind of sex education works best, and at what age? Is it desirable, or even possible, to help a sixteen year old with the anxieties Kathy records here, or is it best simply to let them work out their own solutions?

The authors Kathy remembers from the library are, of course, selected by Ishiguro! So we can expect them to have some thematic relevance. Thomas Hardy, Edna O'Brien and Margaret Drabble all tend to write from the point of view of female protagonists, who are constrained by the society they live in, which disapproves of and controls of them. It may be useful to see Kathy as a heroine in a line which we can draw forwards from Hardy's Tess of the D'Urbervilles. Elsewhere, at the Cottages, Kathy and the others read James Joyce. He is an early user of a "modernist" style, in which a novel consists of little action but is narrated as a "stream of consciousness"- a supposedly unmodulated outpouring of thoughts and memories. Similarly, "Never Let Me Go" can be placed in this literary tradition. It is the absence of much of a conventional plot which makes Kathy's narrative work; the lack of plot, in the sense of a storyline which moves forwards steadily in time, underlines the compromised lives, and the absence of a future, which

Hailsham students (and all clones) face. After Tommy has died, Kathy can only really look backwards. Her memories will have to compensate for the experiences she has not had and will never have.

Kathy also refers to "The Great Escape", a 1963 film about Allied prisoners planning their escape from a prison camp. Hailsham is a prison, in the sense that the woods are out of bounds (chapter 5). The World War 2 camps were discussed at the start of Chapter 7. At the Cottages, the students do not go out because they are unused to freedom- although they always have to return by a certain time and day, set in the ledger (just as Kathy can get a day pass for Tommy, but has to return him by a prearranged set time). In the Steve McQueen film, only three prisoners escape- the rest are shot or recaptured. Perhaps Ishiguro intends us to think that his trio- Kathy, Tommy and Ruth- do achieve a kind of escape, in that they refuse to be as institutionalised as the others, and they can live a more bearable life, emotionally at least, once they have "escaped" to see the washed-up boat, and made up some of their differences.

Being allowed to watch "The Great Escape" over and over again is a little like watching "My Fair Lady"- the underlying message is that there is nowhere to escape to; that escape is futile, because our origins draw us back. We cannot escape our circumstances, and it is a waste of effort to try. The trips to Norfolk and to Littlehampton, in search of "possibles" and deferrals, will prove that this principle is true.

Chapter 9

For the first time, we begin to see that the triangular friendship between Kathy, Tommy and Ruth has the potential to become romantically complicated. Kathy finds herself described by two girls (her friend Hannah, and the less subjective Cynthia) as **the "natural successor" to Ruth**, while she also, as Ruth's friend, tries to negotiate Ruth's reconciliation with Tommy, after they have both been immature regarding sex with other students (in Tommy's case, with Martha H). Kathy defers her own plan for a sexual initiation with Harry C, because, in some way, she would like to hope that Tommy is now available to her.

Kathy's loyalty to Ruth means that she can only talk to Tommy about Ruth. **Tommy is** surprisingly reluctant to recommit himself, because he is not unhappy, and because he is **preoccupied now with what lies beyond Hailsham.** His awareness of the short path to donations makes him realise that just any old relationship is a waste of precious time. It is unfortunate that he does not reject Ruth for Kathy at this point.

This new perspective of Tommy's has come out of his recent meeting with Miss Lucy, at which the guardian had retracted her previous advice, and told him that Tommy must treat **art** as important- "not just **because it's evidence**", but because it will be consoling and fulfilling for him personally. She said, too, that **the Gallery was "much more important than I once thought",** and that the other guardians had been right to stress the importance of creativity. The real reason for this is not that everything can or should go into the gallery, but that, as death becomes imminent, art will be a means of self-expression, and of creating things others can remember you by.

Tommy and Kathy will be misled into overinterpreting the significance of the gallery, thinking that it can be used to secure them more time for themselves, in the form of a "deferral". For now, Miss Lucy's comments about what is important have motivated Tommy to look beyond Ruth, and take a sober view of the future. **This more serious- minded outlook is the first evidence of a more "calm and considered" Tommy – attributes which Kathy herself demonstrates more than Ruth does.**

Tommy's new-found resilience and seriousness is knocked aside, by the sudden departure of Miss Lucy, his mentor. Her leaving presumably discredits her message, in his mind, because, **contrary to his own expressed intention (and, perhaps, to Kathy's hopes), "that very evening" Tommy resumes his relationship with Ruth.**

This is a mistake, in the sense that it shortens the time Kathy and Tommy will have together. Tommy senses that he is not entirely compatible with Ruth, but **the known is more persuasive and easier to accept than the unknown. This is one instance of Ishiguro's observation that we submit to what we do not especially embrace, because we do not have the drive to take the road less travelled.**

Part 2

Chapter 10

Leaving Hailsham for the Cottages is a step into a new world- but it is really a state of limbo which leads only to donations and death.

There is no longer any formal education, because, at the age of 16, the students now know the truth- there is no reason to protect them with the distraction of a lie, a false reality, or an equivocation about their futures. The idea that they should spend two years producing an essay has no focus; such a project is irrelevant in the context of what is to be done to them, and they know it. In the short term, though, **the idea of an essay is like a life raft- a small residual connection with the mother ship of Hailsham, to which they will never go back. As Kathy says, the idea that they will continue their studies is like a comfort blanket.**

The Hailsham students still give no thought to the next and final phase of their lives as carers and then donors- perhaps because that is too difficult to contemplate. They are institutionalised to accept and comply with whatever living conditions they are given. The cold at Hailsham does not bother them enough for them to make a stand over it. Their request for a stock of gas canisters for the heaters is refused, as though Keffers thinks they would "cause an explosion". **The students are refused any opportunity to acquire the equipment of resistance, terrorism (or suicide)- as at Hailsham. Like farm animals, they are living on a run-down farm, in damp, cold, muddy, uncomfortable conditions, and they are not cared for particularly well. The "veterans" will go to the slaughter first; the Hailsham students will take their place, and so the cycle will continue, just as with short-lived farm stock. Kathy is ironically unaware of the parallel, when she tells us that there were "barns, outhouses, stables all converted for us". Kathy recalls that at first the Hailsham teenagers would "move about together", like sheep or cows.**

There is a certain "excitement" to leaving Hailsham behind, and the former pupils have arrived there knowing that there are no more guardians to turn to. They still have no curiosity about their wider environment, seldom going for walks or visiting the nearest village. They have to sign in and out using a "ledgerbook" provided by Keffers, and their movements are not restricted, but the lack of boundaries puzzles them, and takes time to adjust to; to begin with, they feel scared and awkward.

There are hills in the distance. Like the Hailsham woods, they are vaguely menacing. Kathy's narrative says that, over the next two years there, their group of eight became more confident, but they still could not shake off an undercurrent of fearfulness, and a depending on each other for support.

The veteran couples develop mannerisms and body language by copying what they see on television; so does Ruth. Kathy finds some aspects of Ruth's behaviour irritating. One way or another, **the idea that the group from Hailsham can continue to operate as an extended or pseudo-family is beginning to break down.** Ruth taunts Kathy, accusing her of behaving like a baby and refusing to make new friends- although she will not criticise Tommy for exactly the same behaviour. Ruth has always used Kathy to make her feel better about herself.

Kathy had chosen to study the Victorian novel. This gives Ishiguro the opportunity to give her reading some relevance to his own novel. Kathy is reading **George Eliot's last novel, "Daniel Deronda", which features a self-sacrificing hero (like Tommy), a selfish and calculating female protagonist (like Ruth), and- perhaps more significantly- a minority community whose values and morals are uncontaminated, and which is therefore superior in many ways to the larger society which derides and despises it. This is a subtext which**

summarises the Hailsham pupils' place in the society which they serve, and by which they are exploited. They are treated as an underclass because Madame's efforts to argue that there are benefits in treating the clones humanely have been rejected. As readers, we feel uncomfortable with the argument that this group of sixteen year olds should be treated as farm food or fodder; the debate about animal welfare hinges on polarised views- on whether we see animals as stupid and inferior, and therefore of no intrinsic value; or as beings in their own right.

There is something odd about a thirty-one year old woman (Kathy) revisiting the content of an essay she half wrote fifteen years ago. Her thoughts are occupied by the past (old arguments and rounders matches too) because her life is solitary and her friends and contemporaries are dead. The life of a carer involves endless long drives to Dover or Wales, or through featureless landscapes under grey skies. The stops at service stations are lonely and reflective. Even this pale apology for a life will stop in eight months' time when Kathy stops being a carer and becomes a donor.

In her spoken narrative, **Kathy idealises the two years at the Cottages, just as she has idealised Hailsham. In both locations, the students have minimal privacy and they experience no intimacy worthy of the name. Because they have never been encouraged to think for themselves, they**

have a passive, herd mentality. Their communal existence encourages conformity and submissiveness. None of them would contemplate trying to escape. Kathy's observations about the aping of body language from television programmes reinforces our sense that the veterans and the sixteen year olds are immature and deeply conformist.

Kathy cannot see the point of copying the veterans' empty gestures, partly because she has a keener sense of the outside world (which they are yet to experience). Ruth defends herself by accusing Kathy of being too bound up in the closed world of Hailsham which they must now leave behind. Being "fearful" of the wider world makes them all, as Kathy says, **"unable quite to let each other go". These are not only the words of Kathy's tape, and the title of the novel, but a foreshadowing of Tommy's leave-taking of Kathy in Chapter 23.**

Chapter 11

In this chapter, we see the ways in which living at the Cottages is still a little like Hailsham, and also how it differs.

One of the differences is that the teenagers are sexually active, because there is no regime which prevents or discourages it. **Kathy's description of sex is poignantly naïve.** The clones will not be able to have children- they will be put to death first. The novel's narrative presents them as being aware that they are unable to have children, but **it is never clear whether this is a biological fact (have they been sterilised?) or merely a cultural impossibility.** Kathy's perception of sex - that it is animalistic and unemotional - reminds us of Chapter 7, and Miss Emily's mechanistic definition, and her warnings about emotional involvement. **Because the clones will not have the opportunity to develop long-term emotional attachments, they will never do much more than play around at sex in an unsatisfying way.** This recurs in the sexual behaviours of Kathy and Tommy in Chapter 20. **Sex is a life-affirming activity, and it loses much of its power and significance when you are living under a death sentence, as Tommy is. There is something missing in sex for donors, just as they are missing parts of themselves.**

Chapter 11 is concerned with Ruth's efforts to move on from Hailsham, in **the symbolic significance of throwing away her "collection"**. Keffers' initial reaction to Ruth's items- that even a charity shop would not want them- shows us that, even at Hailsham, with what was talked up as the "bumper crop" of sale goods, the students' prized possessions (like Kathy's cassette tape) have value only as an expression of their personal taste and individuality. **That embryonic sense of one's self is of no significance in a world which will soon harvest your organs.** Ruth noticed that none of the veterans who had not been at Hailsham had collections, and she judged them immature- although she cannot see her own immaturity. With hindsight, Kathy revises her judgment and refuses to be critical of Ruth- now that she is dead.

Just as the issue of donations was never discussed frankly at Hailsham, the departure of veterans on short courses which will lead them to leave and become carers is never addressed openly at the Cottages.

The clones have a typical teenage interest in and curiosity about pornographic magazines- "Steve's collection". Kathy's interest in them is not sexual; she reads them, "focusing on the faces". She is not ready to explain herself to Tommy- or to the addressee to whom she is speaking her narrative- but we will find, in Chapter 15 , that she – like the others- has a half-formed idea that the real people they are modelled on themselves have low social status (such as prostitutes). **Kathy cannot achieve intimacy in the relationships she has at the Cottages, so the drive for intimacy attaches itself to the search for some other type of human connection.**

Chapter 12

Chapters 12- 15 relate the trip to Norfolk which begins to establish a closer relationship between Kathy and Tommy. It forms a coherent episode and it gives the central part of the novel momentum and direction. At the end of Chapter 15, Kathy explains to Tommy the real reason for her interest in the magazines in Chapter 11; she feels that her impulsive and overwhelmingly strong sexual urges – which are, in fact, a normal characteristic of adolescence- make it likely that her "model" or "possible" is a sex worker. Ruth and the others have imagined that Ruth's "possible" is an office worker, but, once they have tried to identify her, and realise that there is no match, Ruth's outburst reinforces our awareness that the clones are taken from a sub-class (" Junkies, prostitutes, winos, tramps. Convicts, maybe...."). The world they will die to serve has no interest in their drive for social respectability and to find their origins or any legitimate connection with it.

The Norfolk episode also establishes and explains **the rumour about deferrals** and how it has come about. Clones like Chrissie and Rodney who did not attend Hailsham have somehow come to believe that those who were there have special status and privileges. **Ruth has allowed this misconception to continue, and has encouraged misguided theories for dramatic effect- just as she had encouraged the idea that her pencil case had been given to her by Miss Geraldine, as a token of her specialness,** not bought at the sales (see Chapter 5).

The truth about the gallery only emerges in Chapters 21 and 22. Tommy knows that there is no evidence to support the theory that the children's art was collected as a way of evaluating their capacity for true love, but, as his relationship with Kathy develops, he will allow himself to believe in this optimistic fantasy. The non-Hailsham students have fallen for **the myth that Hailsham is a gilded place of magical privilege. This is neat on Ishiguro's part because it echoes a belief among some sections of our own society that a private or fee-based education somehow confers on its students some special status- that it creates an elite whose chances of survival in the wider world are better than those of the rest. In fact, this, too, is not true, but it is tempting to think it might be, if you are on the outside looking in- as Chrissie and Rodney and the others are.**

Miss Lucy's unexplained reversal of her earlier advice to Tommy- saying, finally, that art was, after all, of great importance- makes his false assumption, that their art is collected for a more noble purpose than merely to justify marginally humane treatment up to the age of sixteen, natural and understandable.

Just as Kathy, with the magazines, and Tommy, with the art he has started to produce, are looking for ways to assert their place in the world and establish their own identity, Ruth is obsessed by the idea that her original is working in an open-plan office in Cromer. Ishiguro reveals for the first time that **"each of us was copied…from a normal person". It is natural to want to find this person, or at least to look for them- as adopted children look for their biological parents.**

In Chapter 12, Kathy explains at some length that she felt that Chrissie wanted to establish a close enough friendship with Ruth to try to trigger a deferral- she thought that Ruth must know the procedure. The identification of Ruth's "possible" in an open-plan office mirrors, suspiciously closely, her imagined "dream future", which, pathetically, she had derived from a soggy magazine insert dropped on a muddy path.

The veterans who have started to train as carers- and who therefore know that no career in offices or shops or as a driver is possible for anyone- simply walk away when the younger and newer residents start to imagine that they will have any individual or personal choice . But this escapism is harmless for a short time- it demands that they deliberately disregard much of what they already know about caring and then donating. Such an act of forgetting is possible, in a new location, after Hailsham and Miss Lucy are in the past. **These conversations remind us of Chapter 7, where Miss Lucy confronted the children with the truth about their future lives.**

Chapter 12 ends with a clear understanding in the reader's mind that the trip to Norfolk- the "lost corner"- will include Ruth's obsessive search for identity, and begin to explore the theory that special privileges have applied to Hailsham students.

Chapter 13

The opening paragraphs convey the strength of Ruth's desire to find her possible. When they stop, an hour into the journey, she "was **gazing across the field at the sunrise**"- **as if the trip promises a dramatic new beginning.**

The description of what Kathy noticed in Cromer, and particularly the cardboard sign in the café, is pointedly childlike and naïve. Rodney and Chrissie want to evade the search for Ruth's possible. Their apparent motive for the trip is to visit their old friend Martin, who is now a carer- even though **visiting carers is discouraged** and "naughty" **(which explains Kathy's chronic isolation, after a decade as a carer). Their real motive is to find out from Ruth how to apply for a deferral**; they cannot interrogate her properly about this on home soil, in case others adopt the same plan. Ruth is desperate to ingratiate herself with Rodney and Chrissie because they alone know where her possible is to be found. She has, therefore, failed to put the record straight about rumours that Hailsham students have gone on to work in shops or as a park-keeper, escaping the carer-donor track. Tommy is "bewildered" at this invention, because of his strong drive for honesty and truth.

Chrissie confronts the others with the central myth about Hailsham- that its former students can obtain a deferral from donations for three or four years if they can prove that they are in love and in a heterosexual relationship. It is purely hearsay among non-Hailsham pupils, but **merely putting the idea on the table creates "a kind of tingle"**.

Because Ruth wants to be shown where her possible is, she condones and reinforces the false notion of the deferrals- **"they told us a few things, obviously" is an outright lie**. Tommy's honesty almost torpedoes Ruth's lie, but Ruth discredits him and maintains her cool deception. The awkwardness described in the final sentence of the chapter shows us that Ruth's inability to provide the details of a non-existent application process will cause tension and conflict.

Chapter 14

Perhaps because Ruth has failed to divulge the application process for deferrals, Rodney is in no hurry to lead Ruth to her possible. Instead, they take a detour into Woolworth's to buy "really cheap" birthday cards. Woolworth's was a chain of high-street shops which went out of business at the end of 2008.

Kathy tells her listener that she still likes shops like these, where you can browse and "hang around". It seems that **carers have no money to spend** on anything except the bare essentials. Similarly, at the Cottages, as at Hailsham, supplies are delivered but there is no sense that the residents have money to spend on shopping or entertainment; Kathy seems never to have been to a cinema, a theatre or a concert. In economic terms, the former students are in a similar position to convicted prisoners in our social system. They are housed and given the means to feed themselves (stew), but money is not allocated for anything beyond their basic upkeep (hence the search for the cheapest possible birthday cards). This is true of Kathy's career as a carer, too- she does not have money to spend in the shops, or for indulgences.

Kathy overhears Ruth still fuelling Chrissie's false belief that there is a procedure for securing a deferral; Ruth knows that she is lying, and resents Kathy for hearing her.

The search for the possible is satisfactory at first, because there is some apparent similarity between the woman and Ruth; but Ruth wants to go back for a second inspection and in the meantime the possible emerges. **They follow her into the art gallery**. After closer inspection, they agree that the superficial resemblance is only that; the link is a false one. **It is ironic that it is in the context of the gallery that Ruth's hopes and dreams are dashed; in the same way, Tommy and Kathy will have their own dream destroyed when they visit Madame at the house where she has kept her gallery.** There is a further irony in that Kathy says she has been back to this building and that it is no longer a gallery, but a shop. Galleries do not survive.

Kathy finds that the sea themes of the paintings in The Portway Studios induce a dream-like condition of "sheer peacefulness", but being in the same room as the possible and hearing her conversation dispels the idea of a connection with Ruth: reality destroys dreams of closeness or connectedness with the world clones are denied a place in.

Near the start of Chapter 13, they had stood on the road, and seen "zigzagging footpaths" leading down to the sea. As they return to the car, they see the same paths, but now they lead down to a promenade "with **rows of boarded-up stalls"- a detail symbolic of the dead ends this excursion has led both the Hailsham students and the veterans to.**

The others try to manage Ruth's disappointment over the mismatch (which was like looking for a needle in a haystack- almost certain to be an impossible quest). But Chrissie and Rodney are "relieved" that Ruth has not found a match which might lead her- like the supposed shop worker and park-keeper- to an alternative, "privileged" life. Ruth's bitter disappointment emerges in her assertion that clones belong "in the gutter". Kathy refuses to join in the illicit visit to the carer, Martin. This leaves her and Tommy time to find a replacement for Kathy's lost tape in a second-hand shop.

Kathy and Tommy try to help Ruth to cushion her disappointment and they both line up on the side of the rational, rather than the emotional. This foreshadows the final conversation, in which Kathy and Tommy discuss and agree about the differences between them and Ruth; Tommy and Kathy are brave and curious to reach the truth- whereas Ruth has a need to fantasise, because she cannot accept the reality of her situation. She wants to believe that deferrals really do exist.

Chapter 15

Ruth's absence for an hour makes time and space for Kathy and Tommy to search for the lost tape, and to exchange some secrets- for Kathy, her insecurities about her sexuality; for Tommy, his revived attempts at art, and his theory about the Gallery as a test of the soul's capacity for true love.

As readers, we side with the underdogs, and so we would like there to be some escape from the profound cruelty of the death sentence these characters live under. The prospect of an hour rooting through junk shops is elating for Kathy- "fun and laughter".

Tommy knows that there is no evidence that a deferral scheme exists. Perhaps **the finding of Kathy's tape encourages a false optimism.** Tommy has thought extensively about unexplained events at Hailsham, and he reveals a concept or idea which is new for us- that the paintings in the Gallery "revealed ...your soul". The Gallery was examined in Chapter 3, where it was clear that it was highly selective; and the tokens issue is in Chapter 4, where Miss Lucy had refused to explain the "important" reason for the Gallery. The grim truth is that the Gallery merely secured Hailsham as it was, and "protected" its students from an even more compromised life. **The revulsion and dread of the clones which Madame demonstrated at the end of Chapter 3 informs Ruth's comments about the gallery attendant at the end of Chapter 14; no-one would knowingly talk to a clone.**

Tommy possesses a degree of humanity which leads him to a judgment that the Gallery must have a humane purpose. He wants to find the replacement tape for Kathy, to show that he cares about her. In this chapter, the compatibility which had made Kathy the natural successor to Ruth for Tommy (chapter 9) resurfaces, because of Ruth's short absence from the narrative. Tommy tells Kathy that Ruth has persuaded herself that deferral is possible and that she will "want to apply ". As Kathy says, a Tommy without art would then be of no use to Ruth. Tommy seems motivated more by the need to create art than the prospect of being with Ruth. This reminds us that at the end of Chapter 9 his commitment to Ruth was underwhelming.

Tommy acknowledges that the desire to find out who you are cloned from is natural, but needs to be resisted, to avoid sensing how futile your life is, as a clone. He is similar to Kathy in his lack of sentimentality. He steers Kathy away from the presumption that her model is a sex worker.

The return journey sees Ruth realigning herself with Kathy, now that her need to have her curiosity satisfied by the information only Rodney had has gone. It is **only Kathy** who **does not have an emotional need to believe in the possibility of deferral, because she is the only one of these five who is not in a relationship.**

Chapter 16

After the trip to Norfolk, the narrative returns to the slow pace of life at the Cottages- a cycle of veterans leaving (to train and work as carers) and newcomers arriving, as the Hailsham students had, the previous summer; but there are no arrivals from Hailsham now. Oddly, those staying behind see leaving the Cottages as something desirable, because it promises "a bigger, more exciting world"- a view which ignores the fact that it is another irreversible step towards the acute pain of donation and death. Understandably, rumours about deferrals become stronger, as a form of wish-fulfilment or escapism; and it is said that it is not only Hailsham students who can secure delays.

Tommy shows Kathy his drawings of imaginary animals; Ruth has seen them, a week earlier. **They correspond with Tommy's personality ("sweet, even vulnerable")**. Kathy does not praise them, because she does not know how to judge them, but she agrees that there is no good reason why Tommy should keep his drawing a secret.

Ruth develops selective amnesia about Hailsham- possibly because she does not want to be associated with the deferrals procedure. Some weeks earlier, Ruth had seen Kathy's replacement tape, and she was surprised and disturbed that neither Kathy nor Tommy had mentioned it to her- as though they were keeping it as their secret. Laughing about Kathy's recently departed boyfriend leads them on to laughing about Tommy, and laughing about Tommy's art.

Kathy is relieved that Ruth does not see Tommy's drawings as the means to applying for a deferral. A few days later, Ruth points out that Tommy has only just told her about his theory about the Gallery- another secret he has shared with Kathy. Ruth's insecurity leads her to tell Tommy that Kathy regards his drawings as a joke- a move about which Kathy says "I had no idea........how far-reaching the repercussions would be". It can only undermine Tommy's trust in Kathy. So, too, does Kathy's reaction- leaving without trying to explain what had happened, or why. Tommy has no reason to believe that Kathy thinks his art is good.

Chapter 17

Chapters 17-19 relate the loosening of the old dynamics which had allowed **Ruth** to be bossy and inconsiderate to Kathy and Tommy. She **redeems herself by acknowledging that she has always stood in the way of what would have been a much better relationship- between Kathy and Tommy**. She relinquishes Tommy, encouraging Kathy to apply to Madame for a deferral with him (she has, somehow, obtained Madame's address); then, on her second donation, she dies.

The relationship between Tommy and Ruth (like Chrissie and Rodney's) has fizzled out under the pressure of moving away, but Kathy reflects that it was weakening even in the later time at the Cottages. This comes as no surprise after we have read in Chapter 16 about **Ruth's controlling and sarcastic behaviour** towards Tommy. The Hailsham era had ended with **Tommy** expressing reservations about his relationship with Ruth, but he **has been passive** in continuing with it at the Cottages. The reader will also remember from that chapter Cynthia's idea that Kathy is the natural successor to Ruth as a partner for Tommy.

Chapter 17 shows us Kathy trying to maintain her friendship with Ruth, even though Ruth's rejection of much of their shared experience at Hailsham now makes this difficult. Ruth regrets being so scathing about Tommy's drawings, and she concedes that her own relationship with Tommy may not last.

Then she launches a verbal attack which feels like a stabbing of Kathy. She offers the opinion that Kathy may have been wondering about the possibility of a romantic future with Tommy, but she claims that Tommy would never consider the possibility. **She goes on to accuse Kathy of a degree of past promiscuity which he disapproves of. This is an extra twist of the knife. It is also a hypocritical lie,**

because, on the trip to see the boat (Chapter 19) Ruth admits that she was, herself, unfaithful to Tommy at the Cottages with "at least three" other boys.

There is no excuse for this extreme unpleasantness, except for Ruth's insecurity over Tommy. But if she has faced up to the likelihood that their relationship will end- as she says she has- she has no right to speak for Tommy or to impose exclusions on his future freedom of choice.

Ruth's denial of her memories of Hailsham is "so false" that, coupled with her personal aggression, towards Tommy in the previous chapter and towards her now, **Kathy decides that the** era of the post-Hailsham **friendship is at an end. Kathy applies to start working as a carer**, and she keeps Ruth and Tommy at a distance, because they seem to have so much less in common than before. This makes an effective and timely end to Part 2 of the novel.

Chapter 18

After Hailsham and the Cottages, the final section of the novel deals with the deaths of Ruth, Tommy and others. **Kathy's horizons close in, as what she has valued disappears from her life**. She is completely aware of what will happen to her- she will follow the path she has seen so many donors taking- and her leave-taking of the chronically ill Ruth and Tommy prepares her for her own exit from the novel, and her death, which the reader is left to imagine.

In these final chapters, the last sixth of the novel, **Ishiguro examines the need for those who are soon to die to resolve past frictions and set aside petty differences and rivalries.** Donors have no choice over the timing, manner or method of their deaths, and we are conscious of how limited and constrained their experiences have been. They have, though, a singular dignity and courage, and a striking lack of self-pity. This will resonate with readers who face the prospect of an *eventual* death which is probably less grim, because it is not *dying by appointment*.

Kathy explains to the person who is listening to her spoken narrative that being a carer is draining and lonely; it is characterised by a lack of companionship. We know that social visits to carers are not permitted (Chapter 14). **Carers are in their own death's waiting room; they are giving palliative care only to people/clones who will not be living for much longer; and they have their own fate to reconcile themselves to. This explains the otherwise apparently illogical desire Kathy and others have, to move on to the fatal phase of becoming a donor. A long spell as a carer makes your own death desirable, because it will end the zombie-like exhaustion, and because, as Tommy puts it, it fulfils the purpose of their lives. It is truly awful that Kathy and Tommy long for the suffering and

the undignified death which they have already seen so many of their friends and fellow students subjected to by this compassionless society.

Kathy provides supporting evidence in her account of her accidental meeting with Laura (who had always been a comedian at Hailsham, but has now lost her sense of humour completely) seven years on from the Cottages. Laura suggests that Kathy should become **Ruth's** carer, because she had had " a really bad first donation"; her **need for comfort among people she had been familiar with should outweigh the fact that Ruth's bossy and controlling behaviour had alienated her from all of her old friends.**

The parting of Laura and Kathy involves an acknowledgment of the lasting power of Hailsham, despite its closure; it is a symbol of a more humane and dignified way of life which they once shared, and which continues to define, or at least influence, their values. Kathy reflects that the closure of Hailsham seems odd, and "unnerving". The reader will understand that it is disturbing because Hailsham was the only significant symbol of humanity and civilisation. The young pupils will have been redistributed to institutions "a far cry from Hailsham"- places where there are no guardians, and no protection from knowing too much too soon. The Hailsham dream has died.

Once Kathy realises that Hailsham's closure represents the end of an era, it concentrates her mind; **she decides to go to help Ruth, because time is short.**

This sense of urgency and clarification because time is short raises, subliminally- in our minds, if not Kathy's- the question of deferrals, because the last time they were discussed, in Chapter 15, Tommy had let pass the practical difficulty of there being no known application procedure, saying that **"we've got time. None of us are in any particular hurry".**

The last part of Chapter 18 records Kathy's first visit- and subsequent ones- to Ruth. Kathy's language is a shade surreal, in the context of caring for someone who is being progressively put to death- "she told me…that my hair suited me". There is a dramatic moment where Kathy realises that Ruth "didn't trust me", demonstrated "a real wariness", and anticipated, with a "look of alarm", that Kathy had come "to do something to her"- to exact some form of reprisal for Ruth's past cruelty to her. This change is Ruth's attitude is prompted by two things- her physical weakness, and her desire to be forgiven before she dies. We will only find that out towards the end of Chapter 20. Fearfulness has taken the place of some of her old assertiveness and aggression.

Ruth wants to see Tommy, whom she has not seen since the time at the Cottages. We know, from the previous chapter, that this is seven years earlier than Kathy's spoken autobiography- the text of the novel. The tale of the stranded boat- which donors at various recovery centres have enjoyed an excursion to see-gives her and Kathy the opportunity to visit it, and take Tommy. Ruth confirms to Kathy that their relationship had already run its course when they left the Cottages to train as carers.

Chapter 19

The Kingsfield Centre, Tommy's home, is a rather grim converted seaside holiday camp. As early as the second paragraph of the chapter, Kathy lets slip that "later on" it became "familiar and precious"- a hint that she will be closer to Tommy than ever before. It is really a detention centre; no holiday camp at all.

When they arrive, and Ruth is still in the car while Tommy and Kathy greet each other, the emphasis is, again, on Ruth's discomfort- " a serious, almost frozen look". Kathy uses the analogy of Tommy and her acting in a performance which Ruth has to watch. If this were narrated from Ruth's point of view, she would be realising that Kathy is indeed her natural successor as Tommy's girlfriend.

The drive to the boat is, as the **landscapes always are** in this novel, through blank scenery, with no traffic, on a cold day, with grey, cloudy skies. Ruth and Tommy are both self-conscious. Ruth has " a gentle smile", as she tells a long story about a donor, trying to capture Tommy's interest; but Kathy loses patience with the tale, and Tommy says that he was thinking precisely what Kathy said. They are on the same wavelength; Kathy feels a rare moment of elation at the connection. Ruth's expression becomes absent, because she knows that Tommy is finally lost to her.

Tommy and Kathy support Ruth when she panics over the barbed wire on the walk to the boat. Her physical frailty, and their unspoken consciousness that she is now the powerless one in their trio, prompts them to support **and help her, in contrast to the way she had behaved towards them in the churchyard in Chapter 16.**

As the woods thin out and the boat becomes visible, the landscape is characterised by **"ghostly dead trunks" and a watery sunlight,** as though the darkness of death is to be found here and must be discussed. As the ground becomes too boggy to walk on, Kathy sits on **a "dead tree trunk"** and the other two sit on another, **"hollow** and more emaciated than mine". The boat has faded from blue to white, the colour of a skeleton, and its timber is rotting. **This physical context of death and decay prompts the characters to reflect not on their own impending deaths but on the fate of Hailsham and of others. Ruth recounts a recent dream**, in which she is inside Hailsham, watching items of litter passing by outside, carried on a flood.

This is significant because **it anticipates very closely the final paragraph of the novel**. There, Kathy is in Norfolk, looking at the landscape under another grey sky. She stops at a barbed wire fence; the fence catches all manner of litter. She feels that in this lost corner in Norfolk she will be able to rediscover all the people and hopes she has lost or given up, and that Tommy can somehow come back to life here.

For both Ruth and Kathy, this vision of accumulated rubbish is a symbolic moment of perspective, where they step outside of their own lives. **The rubbish is the material of their lives (which have been, materially or economically, poor) and it is a poor return or summation of even a short lifetime's experience, but it is all any of them has.**

Ruth says that Chrissie died during her second donation. She is angry about the secrecy; there is no disclosure to donors of how many of their fellow donors die earlier than they are expected to. She objects to the idea (Rodney's) that Chrissie would not have minded dying prematurely; **Ruth** sees donation as "trying to cling onto life", and her flash of aggression here shows that she **is not herself ready to die**. She attacks Kathy on the grounds that she is still a carer and cannot know how donors feel, but Tommy refuses to side with Ruth. Tommy will use the same argument against Kathy, when he wants her to give up being his carer, to spare her having to see his undignified final struggles.

On the return journey, Kathy makes a point of agreeing with Tommy and disagreeing with Ruth. Kathy stops the car so that they can look at a poster which depicts an open-plan office rather like the one Ruth had dreamed of working in (Chapter 12). Kathy forces Ruth to acknowledge that she remembers the original picture, and she criticises her for not having asked to be allowed to have an office job instead of becoming a carer for five years. Tommy joins in, and the onslaught on Ruth is unfair, because there was no actual possibility of Ruth contacting Madame to ask for special treatment. But Tommy and Kathy are indeed beginning to share an unspoken hope - that exceptions can be made to the rules- just as the late Chrissie and Rodney had, in Chapter 13. The taunting of Ruth here is a well-judged retaliation for her nastiness to Kathy and Tommy in the churchyard in Chapter 16.

Kathy and Tommy can attack Ruth like this because of Ruth's physical weakness and her lack of resilience, but Kathy still expects her to retaliate, to launch an attack, to try to get the upper hand, as she has always done. But, **in the face of a verbal attack of the type Ruth has always been an expert at, she turns the tables on Kathy in a new way, by not lashing out, but by asking her for forgiveness.**

Ruth explains that she had been wrong to imply that Kathy's sexuality was any different from anyone else's; wrong to maintain that she herself was not promiscuous, and wrong to have prevented her from enjoying the relationship she deserved with Tommy, for so long. She seeks redemption through having found Madame's address for them, so that Kathy and Tommy can seek a deferral, even at this late stage.

Kathy's initial reaction is that it is far too late to rescue anything- Tommy has already made two donations, and his health is not conducive to suddenly developing new, deep relationships; **intimacy in the shadow of death is tinged with regret**, as Kathy observes in Chapter 20. But even on the drive back to Dover, after returning Tommy to the Kingsfield, Kathy senses some hope- " a door open to somewhere better".

Having let Tommy go, Ruth can be genuinely Kathy's close friend again, and they have a few months of reminiscences and peace before Ruth's early death.

Ruth asks Kathy, periodically, if she will become Tommy's carer- shorthand for seeking a deferral. Ruth dies three days after her second donation (not on the operating table, as in the film); **the description of her death is one of the most distinguished and unsettling parts of the novel.** The end of Chapter 19 marks Ruth's exit from the novel and it leaves Tommy and Kathy to establish their own relationship and seek out the truth about the referral rumour.

This chapter offers some grotesque echoes of the trip to Cromer in Norfolk. Ruth is isolated, as she was when her "possible" disappointed. The connection between Tommy and Kathy is clearly stronger than any Ruth has with him, and she has to let go of her dream all over again. Moreover, Kathy and Tommy goad her over her failure to pursue the idea of working in an office, on the basis that she told everyone she was entitled to special treatment. It is as if Kathy and Tommy are now playing the parts Chrissie and Rodney had done; and there is talk of

Chrissie, who has died during her second donation- as Ruth is about to.

The Norfolk trip had ended with Ruth trying to compensate for her previous bad behaviour, in being impatient with Kathy and Tommy and sucking up to the others. Here again, she has to put things right with her true friends- this time, by asking for forgiveness and offering Madame's address.

Chapter 20

This chapter is shorter than most of the others towards the end of the novel. It establishes the relationship between Kathy and Tommy, and, under the threat that Tommy may at any time receive notice of his fourth- and final- donation- there is real urgency now to confront the referral issue.

Kathy makes their relationship sexual, not because she feels an intense romantic love for Tommy, but because she feels it is the right thing to do; **the absence of such intimacy might be a tell-tale sign which would mean they fail the deferral test.** As usual, the language Kathy uses to describe anything to do with sex is immature and rather uncomfortable to read.

Despite the unappealing environment of the former holiday camp, Kathy finds this time happy and fulfilling; she arrives in the afternoons (as Tommy's carer), and reads aloud from paperback books. Tommy draws his animals, and rests, and they have "proper sex", although it is "tinged with sadness" because the opportunity has come to them "too late", through the way Ruth had managed to monopolise Tommy for so long. Tommy's physical injuries and the post-operative environment do not help.

When Tommy asks Kathy which of his draft drawings is the best, he is showing her that he is ready to prepare a plan for the quest for a deferral. Kathy detects in the drawings a lack of freshness. Tommy is battered and abused, and even his drawings lack force and imaginative power- as you would expect. Kathy has misgivings about the project; none of the other donors here talk about deferrals. It is as if **the myth has already died out, but they allow themselves to continue to believe in it.**

Kathy's feelings are a sign to the reader that the quest for a deferral will fail. But it cannot be left- otherwise Tommy will die anyway. Kathy has checked that Madame really does live at the address Ruth had provided; it is in Littlehampton, which is on the coast (like Cromer in Norfolk), but in Sussex.

Kathy is a conscientious observer of the rules, so she has fitted her investigations around her work. She would not break the ban on visiting carers in Chapter 14. There is an opportunity to call there the following week, when Tommy has to go out for "lab tests". Kathy is apprehensive, but she hides it. The visit is to be conducted on the basis that it cannot make their lives worse- Madame has no power to have their donations accelerated. **Our clue to the outcome is in the weather- it does not stop raining while they make this plan. Miss Lucy's disastrous attempt to tell the children what they had not been told- that there would be no career, no achievement, just a herding towards death- was accompanied by similarly heavy rain, in Chapter 7. In this novel, heavy rain accompanies the destroying of dreams.**

Chapter 21

In Chapter 21, Kathy and Tommy make their trip to Littlehampton, follow Madame, and are invited into the house. Even **the journey there is ill-fated**- the car is faulty and Tommy's tests are botched. These details set up the expectation, for us, if not for Tommy and Kathy, that the other part of their mission will fail too.

They see Madame and follow her home. **Kathy remembers following Ruth's possible- another parallel which points to an unsuccessful outcome. Moreover, as they follow her, the sun is setting.**

When Kathy speaks to her, from the garden gate, she feels the same "chill" she had felt when Miss Geraldine's guardians had swarmed around her in Chapter 3. Comparing herself with a spider is another example of Kathy's **repetition here of the language from that earlier episode** ; to non-clones, clones are repulsive and frightening. Madame overcomes her physical revulsion, but she is still almost unable to move, out of fear, as the sun goes down, both literally at sunset at 6 p.m., and as the light is about to go out of the dream of a deferral.

The interior of the house is grave-like in its darkness, with heavy velvet curtains drawn closed, dim table lamps, and no fire. To speak to students is a breach of the rules. Madame is less cold and impassive than she was at Hailsham; Kathy detects compassion in her being on the point of crying- a reminder of how she cried over Kathy's dance with her tape.

Tommy explains his theory about the gallery. Madame already knows it. Tommy offers his drawings, and Madame asks the unknown listener whether they should continue with the discussion. That listener is revealed as **Miss Emily**, but she **is now in a wheel chair, and "frail and contorted"- as if she has made donations of her own.**

Chapter 22

This long chapter has to reveal the whole truth- rather like a murder mystery, where the detective finally reveals who the murderer is, to the surprise of all concerned. **Miss Emily's long monologue takes up most of the chapter**, as she explains the ethos of Hailsham, and the struggle and eventual failure to have clones recognised as being more than subhuman.

The end of this novel has to resolve the loose ends- not just the question of referrals, but the puzzle of why Miss Lucy had to leave, and why Kathy's singing to her tape with a pillow for a baby had affected Madame so deeply.

The fact that Miss Emily is having to sell treasured furniture, in order to service a personal debt arising from Hailsham, is evidence of her good intentions.

Two or three couples each year had sought a deferral while Hailsham was open. The myth was not a new one, and Miss Emily, finding herself unable to stop it from spreading, though that - at least for those who believed in it but never tested it- it was a harmless dream, "a little fantasy".

In fact, **Hailsham itself was a giant deferral**, in the way it protected a select number of child clones from the dreadful truth, and enabled them to have a decent childhood, free of worry about their futures. Tommy's theory that art reveals the soul of the artist is close to the purpose of the gallery, but it was less idealistic- it served to argue the difficult and unpalatable case that the clone children were human, so that they were not so different from those who would kill them for their body parts.

Miss Emily speaks of **"students being reared in deplorable conditions"- a linguistic reference to**

farm animals. Are we, in our society, open to the concept that farm animals have personality, even souls- or is our traditional belief that they are a subspecies which exists for our convenience immovably entrenched?

She mentions other institutions- Glenmorgan House and the Saunders Trust- which shared her belief that clones should not merely serve medical science, because they were intelligent, sensitive, and in no way defective or subhuman. Then she refers to the unauthorised Morningdale experiment, and to unspecified news events and documentary television coverage; taken together, these factors turned public opinion against them. Hailsham has vanished- it was sold as a hotel- and only vast government "homes" now exist to supply the donations programme, with none of the refinement or care which Hailsham and similar premises used to provide.

The Morningdale scandal was an illegal experiment in eugenics which involved using genetic selection to create a blueprint for a new breed or strain of genetically superior children. This was **socially unacceptable, because it threatened the established norms, and it contaminated the argument that clones should be treated as human beings too.**

Ishiguro creates a historical context for the novel here, presenting a fictional alternative to the history we know- his alternative is a history in which science achieved the progress we think of as much more recent, as long ago as in the 1950s, and cancer and other deadly illnesses soon became curable through clone technology. Concern for the welfare of clones would never rival the concern people had for their own families and friends to be cured.

Miss Lucy's belief that the children should be fully informed about the course their lives would take put her at odds with Miss Emily, who knew that **children who were told the truth would lose interest in any education or fun and would take no pleasure in their childhood.** The deception was meant kindly; there are some things children should be kept ignorant of.

Kathy's conversation with Madame about the song on the Judy Bridgewater tape takes place as the early evening light- like hope- continues to fade. Madame explains that she was upset because she saw that the young Kathy, with her tender instincts, was the archetype of a child clinging not to a pillow, but to the values of Hailsham, of innocence and of unachievable dreams, which were, inevitably, about to give way to the atmosphere of the abattoir or the concentration camp.

Even at Hailsham- and, of course, by not being part of a family- the children had no models for intimacy, and, throughout the novel, their physical and sexual attempts at expressing support or affection or love have been clumsy and half-baked. But the generation after Kathy's will be denied even what they were able to develop.

Madame and Miss Emily regard the lives of Hailsham students as glasses which were half-full, not half-empty. The reader regards them as completely empty. Kathy and Tommy and Ruth do not make the calculation at all, because, for them, it is only an academic point.

For the reader, there is a further consideration. **The young Kathy's misreading of a romantic song as the tale of a woman who has had a child against all the odds is a tale of regeneration and hope. The clones, by contrast, are being systematically wiped out.**

Tommy's outburst of rage and frustration on the return journey is like his outburst in Chapter 1, on the North Playing Field, when he is not picked for **football; he shouts and screams an incoherent, frustrated stream of obscenities. This comes from his frustration with Hailsham's hiding of the truth. For Tommy- as Miss Lucy had realised- it is better to know your fate. If he had done, he might not have wasted so much time with Ruth- he might have chosen Kathy in the last year at Hailsham. But the game he has been excluded from this time is not a football match, but life itself. This time, the outburst of swearing and distress yields to Kathy's protective embrace.**

The chapter ends with Tommy conceding that his rage (adapting the poet Dylan Thomas' famous phrase, rage against the dying of the light) may stem from some subconscious knowledge that a clone's life is outrageously unfair; and that, from the earliest age, **he was driven by the need to know and be told, not the need not to know and not to be told.**

Chapter 23

After the mystery has been solved, and all hope denied, all that remains is for Tommy to die, for Kathy to grieve, and for her to prepare for her own lonely death.

Tommy becomes more detached from Kathy, and she feels that he prefers the company of his fellow donors. He **does what Ruth had done, when she was close to the end of her life- he questions the relevance of Kathy's opinions because she is not herself a donor.**

Tommy confides to Kathy that the fourth donation- for which he has been given a date- brings with it not only a kind of social distinction, but an acute anxiety that you may not "really complete"- that real death may not happen until after "you've technically completed", because our consciousness can still feel pain, and even, somehow, observe many more donations being taken from us "until they switch you off". She dismisses this fear as "rubbish.....wild talk".

Tommy later tells Kathy that he wants to have a different carer; he does not want to fall out with her, and he does not want her to have to nurse him through the final debilitated days of his life. He says that Ruth, as a donor, would have understood his reasons; and that Kathy cannot.

As they make a sort of peace, in "the dull light", Tommy suggests to Kathy that it is time for her, too, to move on from being a carer to a donor. Then he tells her his daydream. Like Ruth's dream, it involves water, but Tommy's is about him and Kathy letting each other go. He sees two people in a river with a strong current; the current is pulling them apart, just as Tommy is being dragged towards dying and Kathy is moving at a slower pace. While we may have a strong desire not to experience our last weeks or days alone, in the context of the novel that wish is, like **the desire for a deferral, an impossible dream.** Everyone has to let go of their own life and of those they love.

Neuroscientists are at work today on research to do with reports of dreams which people say they have at the time of near-death experiences. Tommy and Ruth both report dreams which are dominated by water flowing past; Ruth is a spectator of the tide and flow of life, and Tommy has to let Kathy go.

There seems to be a cultural or religious dimension to near-death dreams. Christians often report seeing a bright light at the end of a tunnel; Muslims can see doorways; Hindus can report beautiful rivers. In taking the Hindu version, and making it unsettling, I think he has found an effective metaphor for the end of these lives- there is nothing redemptive or heavenly lying ahead of them, just a giving up of their organs and of whatever else a human being/clone comprises.

The last conversation between Kathy and Tommy is one afternoon in December. Tommy draws a telling distinction between Ruth, who could never face the reality of her situation except obliquely, through the delusion of deferrals and dreams of working in an office, and therefore would have been hit hard to find out that deferrals were just a myth, and them. By contrast, as Tommy says, he and Kathy have never been afraid of finding out the truth.

Kathy feels it is wrong that Ruth, who had done so much harm by keeping Tommy and Kathy apart for so long- in fact, until Tommy's ill-health and impending death casts a haunting shadow over their relationship- should have believed to the end of her life that the damage could be undone. More particularly, though, she feels that the three of them- for so long a trio of friends- should all die knowing the same things. In a sense, Ruth has escaped the consequences of her own selfish behaviour, because she did not have to live with the knowledge that there is no such thing as a deferral.

Tommy's final act with Kathy is not to tell her he loves her, but to share his last undisclosed secret- an unimportant one about how he celebrated scoring a goal in football matches. It, too, features water, which, he used to imagine, was no more than ankle deep- a marked contrast with the irresistible current in the fast-moving river he imagines he and Kathy are in now.

Kathy is now reconciled to a period of solitude, confined as a donor, with no possibility of seeing Hailsham again, or Ruth, or Tommy; she is content to have internalised her memories, so that she has something of her own to derive comfort from during her future pain (just as the dying donor in Chapter 1 had borrowed Kathy's recollections of Hailsham). **She does not believe donors who say that you lose memories as well as parts of your physical self.**

Kathy's only assertion of her own emotional needs, to make her own peace with her thwarted dreams- her only departure from the script- is not a rebellious act, but a final visit to Norfolk, a fortnight after she had heard that Tommy had died. She stood on the edge of a field, kept out by a wire fence entangled with rubbish caught on it, and she reflected on her life. Somehow the power of the imagination still lives on, even in the shadow of death; it creates an alternative or virtual reality, in which Kathy thinks that in Norfolk, the so-called lost corner of England, everything she has lost herself will miraculously come back to her.

This episode links back to the explanation of "our Norfolk theory" in Chapter 6- anything "precious" that was lost could always be recovered by seeking it in Norfolk. While this is true of Kathy's lost tape, it cannot, of course, be true of Tommy.

Barbed wire is the symbol of No Man's Land on the battlefield- a place where helpless soldiers are trapped and murdered. The image of the rubbish is touching, because the lives of the clone children have been treated as if they are rubbish.

On one level, they have never owned anything more valuable than "the collections" which Keffers laughed at.

On another level, they have lived their humble and disregarded lives with courage and dignity.

When we read the novel, we cannot avoid asking ourselves whether we do the same.

The main characters and where to find them!

Kathy or Kath H (only Tommy calls her Kath)

Kathy introduces herself in the opening chapter. She takes pride in her work, and she has various techniques for dealing with donors. She is alert to the possibility that other people are jealous of her, or disapprove of her apparent success and privileges, and her background at Hailsham, with its collegiate and charmed life, and its shared experience, which helped to overcome her differences with Ruth. She knows she can be forceful. In speaking to Tommy, she disobeys Ruth (chapter 1).

She is interested in finding out about the extent of Tommy's troubles. She enjoys reminiscing about Hailsham. She is angry when she thinks Tommy is telling her lies (chapter 2). She is loyal to Ruth even after Ruth has treated her badly (chapter 5), and Ruth has some influence over her (chapters 5 and 6).

From the age of 13, Kathy says that she started asking questions (about her future), even if she did not openly interrogate the guardians; she starts observing Miss Lucy closely (chapter 7).

Ruth says that Tommy respects Kathy because she is brave and she keeps her promises (chapter 9). Kathy herself feels an outsider or a latecomer at Hailsham because of her sexual inactivity (chapter 8). She plans her own sexual initiation carefully and as a project, but then other girls start labelling her Ruth's natural successor as Tommy's girlfriend. She defers her clumsy plan (for Harry C) because she hopes that Tommy will turn from Ruth to her. Kathy's relatively late sexual initiation matches her late coming to the process of being a donor. She is independent-minded; she does not feel peer pressure.

Kathy feels at a disadvantage when she argues with Ruth, in chapter 10 (and in chapter 19). Unusually, in both cases, Kathy uses an analogy to describe her feelings; first, the panic you feel when you realise you have made a potentially disastrous move in a chess game; secondly, when your enemy manages to seize your gun in a film, and glares at you, threatening vengeance because they have the sudden power to do to you whatever they like. Yet- in chapter 11- Kathy makes allowances for Ruth's behaviour which tend to strike us as over-generous.

Kathy's successful search with Tommy for a replacement for her lost tape is much more intensely satisfying than Ruth's approximate substitute; Kathy feels a romantic bond with Tommy (chapter 15). She half accepts that Tommy's theory about the Gallery would help to explain Madame's sadness when she had found Kathy dancing to the original tape; if the pillow were taken as symbolising a lover, not a baby (which clones can't have) the existence of deferrals would make a good context. This is a misinterpretation.

Kathy's discussion of sexuality with Tommy (at the end of chapter 15) is much more genuine than Ruth had been. When she sees his drawings (chapter 16) she describes them as innocent and fragile, rather like him; suggesting to the reader that they do indeed reveal his personality or soul.

Chapter 19 gives Kathy an unfamiliar power over Ruth, because of Ruth's physical and emotional frailty and Kathy's strong alliance with Tommy. Ruth tells her to stay in the car, but Kathy ignores the instruction. Tommy and Kathy taunt Ruth over the dream of working in an office and her tendency not to tell the truth, when it needed to be told.

Kathy feels that it is somehow pointless to attempt a deferral; Tommy's drawings have lost their power, just as he has physically (chapter 20) lost his vitality during the arduous programme of donating organs. She feels not so much outrage or injustice as acceptance at the news that deferrals do not exist.

She finds that she can neither speculate nor provide reassurance when Tommy worries about whether the fourth donation is indeed a complete ending to life and to suffering, or whether there is more cruelty to come. After the event, she wishes that they had discussed it more deeply.

In the end, she feels no hostility to Ruth, although she does not like the fact that Ruth died while she still thought deferrals existed, and did not have to deal with the reality of the legacy she had left Kathy and Tommy.

The final paragraph shows Kathy expressing her grief for Tommy but also facing her own death as resolutely as ever.

Like Tommy and Ruth, Kathy lacks the experience and maturity to deal with complex emotional situations in a mature way. She tends to avoid conflict; she allows Ruth to behave badly for too long. Ishiguro would argue that, in merely living her daily life conscientiously, Kathy is like the rest of us; navigating a small world until our time to die arrives. She fortifies herself against hers with her memories of her friendships and of Hailsham.

Tommy D

At the age of 13, Tommy is continually mocked by other boys, because of his apparent immaturity. He expresses his emotions openly, and is very good at football, which he plays intensely and with great excitement. He is eager when he should be less transparent; when he is not picked to play, he cannot contain his anger and frustration, and he screams and swears on the playing field. Other children label him as lazy because of his perceived lack of effort and creativity (chapter 1).

Kathy thinks his facial expressions and mannerisms are often immature. He has had tantrums, has fought other boys and turned desks over. He is a talented runner, physically large and strong, but he is shunned by other boys, who play unpleasant tricks on him. His facial expressions include smirking (an unattractive or certainly uncomplimentary observation by Kathy), but he becomes less prickly, as he gets older. He can shows that he is approachable (chapter 2). He is inclined to express fear or anxiety in a look (chapter 3); he seems to need time to process his own emotions.

He develops theories, because he has an intuitive capacity for hidden truths which the other characters do not possess (see the end of chapter 22). First is the theory that everything students are told at Hailsham about the future course of their lives is managed and organised with great attention to detail; it is age-specific, and cleverly subliminal. He is also impressionable, and the object of the joke about arms that can unzip. He thinks the other children are showing genuine concern (chapter 7) when they are poking fun at him.

When he is 16, Kathy is concerned that he is regressing and becoming unpredictable, moody and unsociable again (chapter 8). Kathy values consistency and calm. Tommy is twice described as being like thunder. Thunder is difficult to disguise, and it does not see the need to be calm. Tommy's outbursts, at the start and the end of the novel, reflect his particular frustration at falseness.

Tommy is more mature and self-controlled in chapters 8 and 9, because of the influence on him of Miss Lucy. Her sudden departure drives him back to Ruth (back to the old accepted normality) just as he was promising to break away. There is a strong hint in chapter 9 that Tommy, as Miss Lucy predicts, will somehow expose what is secret, and uncover the truths about being a clone. She has already planted in his mind the idea that the gallery gathers some kind of "evidence" and that it is important. Tommy applies original thinking to the question of the purpose of the gallery.

He intuitively detects Kathy's sadness at the end of chapter 11, which means she feels both valued and comfortable with him. He is puzzled and troubled about the half-truths and lies which Ruth allows the veterans to attach to Hailsham (chapter 13). His comments are always direct and he is frustrated at

Ruth's evasions. He has a strong need for honesty. His analysis, that Miss Emily was wrong, in trying to keep uncomfortable truths hidden, while Miss Lucy was right to try to insist on telling the truth, underwrites his preference for being treated as competent to know the truth, rather than being protected or sheltered or kept in the dark.

Although he knows that there was no evidence of a deferral scheme at Hailsham, he allows himself to be carried away by the idea that the Gallery is a selection tool for exactly that (chapter 15)- so much so that he has already started drawing tiny imaginary animals, without telling Ruth.

With Ruth out of the way, Tommy and Kathy finally make their relationship sexual- but, for Tommy, after three donations, it is not completely joyful, because it cannot be carefree; it is too little, too late. The conversation with Madame makes him anxious, and he volunteers his theory about the Gallery.

Miss Emily remembers him as tempestuous, moody, but generous- this could almost be an epitaph. His reaction to the news that deferrals do not exist is delayed- the furious screaming in the field only takes place in a place where no-one except Kathy will hear it. The only consolation is that Kathy can comfort him more effectively now than when he had his outbursts at Hailsham, and he appears to recover composure.

He does not want Kathy to have to care for him as his physical health collapses. Whether he antagonises

Kathy deliberately, by saying that Ruth would understand his feelings, while she cannot (because she is not a donor), is open to interpretation. His analysis, that he and Kathy have always been in love, but have to let go now- shattering the exhortation which gives the novel its title- is firm, brave and unsentimental.

Ruth

Ruth is often critical of Tommy, whom she calls an idiot. Unlike Kathy, she does not wish to help him with his troubles, and she is unsympathetic and critical; she says he needs to be more self-controlled (chapter 1), and that he needs to change his approach. Ruth tends to act as a leader of opinion and she is bossy (chapter 2). It Is her theory that Madame is scared of the students (chapter 3); she is right. At the age of 5 or 6 she had a bad temper; a couple of years later, she has her imaginary horses (chapter 4). She uses the concept of the plot to abduct Miss Geraldine as a source of her own authority or leadership (chapter 5), and she happily gives Kathy the impression she is an expert chess player, although she does even not know the rules. She is callous to people she falls out with (expelling Kathy from the secret guards) but she still inspires loyalty.

These childhood episodes lay the ground for Ruth's later behaviour. She enjoys power, and can be cruel and sarcastic in abusing it. She belittles Tommy and

Ruth, at the Cottages; and other children when they were younger.

Ruth is sufficiently caring to help to search for Kathy's tape, and to give her a substitute (chapter 6). She is, though, obliged to Kathy over her pencil case secret, so her kindness comes out of a sense of obligation, not pure generosity. The same applies to her motivation in chapter 19, when she gives up her claim on Tommy.

She theorises- correctly- in chapter 8 that the sex education at Hailsham is really intended only for use after they have left. She has a serious falling-out with Tommy over his infidelity with other girls- a hypocritical pose, because she does the same herself at Hailsham and at the Cottages. Ruth knows that Tommy will listen to Kathy. Ruth regards her relationship with Tommy as a matter of keeping the score (chapter 9); she is wrong to say that she and Tommy are a perfect and permanent match. She is possessive towards him because she lacks Kathy's inner calm. She uses him to make herself feel better.

Kathy finds much of Ruth's behaviour at the Cottages immature and derivative; false. Ruth's habit of spoiling the plot of novels others are reading is irritating (chapter 10) and a pretence at superiority. She is unpleasant and sarcastic to Kathy at the end of this chapter.

When Kathy seeks reassurance or advice from Ruth over her sexuality, Ruth is anything but helpful; unlike a true friend, she seeks to undermine Kathy's confidence even more. Later, in chapter 19, she admits that she knew exactly what Kathy meant, because her own experience is the same. When Ruth sees a weakness in another person, she exploits it.

Ruth's aggressive way of speaking to Kathy contrasts with her submissive and ingratiating style with Chrissie and Rodney (chapters 12 and 13), which leads to the misconception about special favours for Hailsham students and the existence of deferrals.

Ruth is bitterly disappointed at the unsatisfactory pursuit of her possible, because, as Tommy says in the final pages, she wants to believe that it is possible to escape from the fate of a clone; even if this means making up the theory you then choose to believe in. On the car journey back from Cromer, Ruth has to make her peace with Kathy and Tommy- a foreshadowing of the trip in chapter 19.

Soon, Ruth is irritating Kathy again by denying things to do with Hailsham which she cannot have forgotten; she reacts badly (out of jealousy and possessiveness) when she finds out that Kathy's tape had been replaced, and that neither Tommy nor Kathy had told her. Ruth exacts revenge by telling Tommy, hurtfully, that Kathy had laughed at his drawings (chapter 16). Her motive is to keep Tommy and Kathy apart, even though she herself is now less close to him- there is no suggestion that they will apply for a deferral as a couple.

Ruth's final insult at the Cottages is to tell Kathy that Tommy would never have her as his girlfriend because of her promiscuity - an outrageous lie. In telling it, she destroys the last shreds of their identity as a trio of friends. When Kathy becomes her carer, Ruth is guarded, because she expects some form of revenge to be taken on her (chapter 18). She has a guilty conscience.

Ruth orchestrates the boat trip in chapter 19, so that she can apologise to Kathy and Tommy for keeping them apart, apologise for her lies, and give them Madame's address, with the legacy (because she is herself almost dead) that they are to seek a deferral for themselves. Ruth's responses to stimuli in this chapter – her gestures, expressions and body language, and her language- add up to a deathbed confession of guilt and shame. Combined with the painful death she suffers two pages later, she is rehabilitated, at least in part; for all her faults, she has finally tried to make amends.

Madame

She is French or German, not very feminine in appearance, and with a distancing, cold expression (chapter 3). When Kathy speaks to her, outside her house, she reacts with a cool, severe look, as though something had been thrown at her. She "stiffen(s)", but then overcomes her "revulsion". She no longer seems a "hostile stranger"; she sounds almost "sarcastic", and she is crying (again). She addresses Tommy and Kathy as "poor creatures"; her tears are of sorrow and compassion, because they are deceived in their hopes of special treatment. Then someone calls her "Marie-Claude". It is Miss Emily, who also calls her "darling", and says that she has become "disillusioned" with the Hailsham project.

She finally explains to Kathy that her sadness and tears over the tape at Hailsham came from the knowledge that the world would be cruel and heartless to children like Kathy.

Miss Emily

The head guardian; she appears haughty; has silvery hair, tied back, and speaks slowly and carefully. She is intimidating, but she also makes the children feel safe. She sometimes uses language they do not understand, has an uncanny skill of knowing where a child may be hiding, and she rarely issues punishments (chapter 4). Although she is a figure of authority, she is acutely compassionate to the children- which is why, in her view, Miss Lucy has to leave Hailsham.

She reappears at the very end of chapter 21, frail, contorted and wheelchair-bound. She explains the demise of Hailsham and the true purpose of the gallery. She is dispassionate, with a "thin smile" and "narrowed eyes". She defends the Hailsham project because of the better quality of life it enabled its students to have, even though it has finally failed and, once its last students like Kathy have died, it will be more or less forgotten.

Major themes

Kathy, Tommy, Ruth, their fellow students at Hailsham, and many other children in less pleasant homes, all exist for one reason only- to be organ donors who will not survive much beyond the age of 30. They will die while their lives are still incomplete, and, from a young age, they cannot avoid knowing that they will be put to death at a prematurely young age.

The most prominent themes grow out of these basic truths in the novel. You need to think, in particular, about the following-

-the importance of fear

-friendship

-intimacy

-death

-the role of hope

-the importance of memories

These themes reflect Ishiguro's stated aim, of using the novel to examine the question "What really matters to you when you know you have only a short time to live?".

He is less interested in some broader social and ethical issues which may strike us as sub-themes (concepts of society, individual rights and freedom, the way we treat minorities, the implications of scientific and medical discovery). While literary critics will be interested in making inferences about these topics, it is the major themes we should concentrate on for GCSE.

If you have read the novel closely, and read this guide carefully, you will have your own ideas about these themes. Here is a summary to help you to gather your thoughts on each of the SIX major themes listed above.

The importance of fear

The ethos and aim of Hailsham is to stop its children from feeling fear, except in the sense that they know that they must not leave the premises; there are terrifying stories about anyone who has dared to go into the woods in the past.

Miss Emily uses Hailsham as a means to allow some clones as normal a childhood as possible. If its students are given some education, it will be apparent that they are not merely dumb animals, or creatures with no soul and no value. A happy childhood is one without fear, or constant thoughts of death. Miss Lucy is dismissed from Hailsham because she believes it is dishonest to hide from the students the awful truth of what awaits them in the remainder of their short lives. As they look back at their Hailsham years, Kathy and her friends value the protection it gave them; because they were not oppressed with thoughts of their own death, they could make friendships, and express their individuality and creativity.

Some of the most effective writing in the novel shows us Ruth's fear of dying. Tommy is unafraid of death, but he is afraid of the possibility that, in some tortured and passive form, life may continue beyond the fourth donation. Kathy shows a remarkable absence of fear, but she has not yet become a donor. We tend to feel that, when she does, she will approach the project more like Tommy than like Ruth. Ruth was selfish, and she was always afraid to confront reality; Kathy and Tommy are unselfish, and their drive for honesty and truth makes them better equipped to face their own deaths without the same degree of fear.

Madame is afraid of the cloned children, because she regards them as sub-human (although she feels sorry for them).

Ruth is interested in the idea of escaping into a recognisably normal life- working in an office. Her strong drive to find the person from whom she was cloned, and her belief in the concept of deferrals- which leads her to be dishonest with herself, and with

Rodney and Chrissie- both show that she is afraid to accept the truth, that there is no escape.

Friendship

The children have not been born naturally- they have been manufactured- and so they have no biological or adoptive families. The guardians are less formal in many ways than orthodox teachers, but they are not permitted to become too friendly with the students. The discussion in Cromer informs us that carers like Kathy are not permitted to make friendships among themselves; and their relationships with donors are relatively short-term and detached. Whereas we are used to having new groups of friends at different times in our lives, the childhood friendships formed among the students at Hailsham are more or less all there will ever be for them. Their attempts at forming romantic relationships are often transitory and experimental.

Friendships formed at Hailsham are therefore particularly important to the main characters, because they will not have an opportunity to improve upon them in their shorter times as veterans and then donors.

Kathy relates the difficulty of making the adjustment from being at Hailsham to being at the Cottages; the Hailsham students cannot simply continue to operate as an exclusive group, but they find it hard to make real friends with people whose background and upbringing lacks the privileged education they have had.

During the time at the Cottages, Ruth behaves badly towards Kathy, who remains loyal to her because she is her oldest friend, and because, as a six year old, Kathy was in awe of Ruth's social dominance and power. The dynamics of the relationship between Kathy and Ruth become very important to the structure of the novel; Ruth's apology only has emotional force because she has been such a bad friend to Kathy, and the lateness of it- it is too late for Tommy and Kathy to have the kind of relationship they should have had years earlier- has dramatic power.

Madame and Miss Emily are a same-sex couple, who share a vision or mission (though it has been defeated) and understand each other; they occupy the same house and their relationship is tolerant and relaxed whereas Ruth is controlling and tense with Tommy.

Ruth manages, briefly, to achieve a deeper friendship with Kathy, but only when she is waiting in Dover to undergo her fatal second donation.

Being a veteran is not conducive to making friends; the emphasis at that time of life is on sexual exploration. As a donor, Tommy has no close friends- only Kathy- and the profession of carer isolates Kathy from a social life- she has little energy for it, and carers are not authorised to make friendships.

The role of intimacy

Just as the students are groping for an understanding of what they do not know (about donation and completion and deferrals), they are, to borrow Miss Lucy's favourite phrase, told and not told about sex, sexuality and relationships. The sex education at Hailsham (in Miss Emily's lectures) raises more questions than it answers and the students are confused about how they should behave sexually.

Kathy's sexual behaviour at the cottages is very hit and miss. Her plan to practice sexual technique with Harry C lapsed. She has waited all her short life for Tommy, but her sex life with him is described in an unexcited way. Because it comes too late, and because he is so unwell, it is almost irrelevant. The novel is similar to Shakespeare's "Romeo and Juliet" in that separation- through death, banishment, or a suicide pact- relegates sexual connections between lovers to the margins of life, when they know that they will die soon.

The clone children have the additional handicap that they have no families or role models for successful adult relationships. The feeble attempts of the veterans at the Cottages to copy the behaviour of married couples on television shows that they have no authentic examples to follow. Being part of a couple brings with it the rumours of a deferral (but only for heterosexuals); "love" and sex are, inevitably, bound up, for the clone, with death and the desire to delay it.

When Kathy relates her conversations with Ruth and Tommy, she seems much younger than 31, but the events she describes are several years old. The clones do not go on to social workplaces or higher education, where they can develop an adult's understanding of people. Neither Ruth nor Kathy can achieve a satisfying level of intimacy with Tommy, because every day is a day closer to the undignified process of completing. Ishiguro does not seek to embarrass his characters for their lack of emotional and sexual intelligence; he simply shows us how these things fall away, as the need to make peace becomes the over-riding drive, in the shadow of death.

Death

Death is rarely mentioned in the novel; the euphemism of completing is the substitute for it. It is both ironic and sad that dying from multiple organ donation is only completion in the sense that it brings misery to an end; it is the end of a lack of fulfilment, and the last stage in the continuing denial that the clone children are as human or normal as those whose illnesses they will die to cure.

Both at Hailsham and at the Cottages, children/clones begin to indulge the harmless fantasy that they will become film stars or shop assistants- that they will live a normal life span. The guardians and the veterans do not want to crush those dreams, but Miss Lucy is not prepared to let the Hailsham students be misled.

Compassion requires that the children are sheltered from the true horror of their predicament.

While Tommy makes light of his bleeding and pain, he expresses his deep-seated fear to Kathy- that even a fourth donation may leave you alive in some way, and defenceless against being stripped of even more of your physical self.

These rumours are persistent enough to have more substance than the concept of deferrals, even though the truth of existence after the fourth donation can never be proved or disproved.

Ruth's partial rehabilitation in the reader's eyes derives largely from the account of her death Kathy gives us at the end of Chapter 19. We understand why Miss Emily is so concerned not to deprive the clones of a more or less happy and carefree childhood, and why the sanitising of death is habitual in the world of donors, but we, like Kathy, know how horrific it really is.

We owe the taboo status our culture attaches to the idea of death to the Victorians, and the Romantics. You will not need to read many Victorian gravestones, or much 19th century poetry, to find the finality of death reduced to the cosy and familiar process of "falling asleep".

The role of hope

For most of us, life will contain a mixture of hopes and fears. Ideally, we wish to live happy, healthy, long lives; no-one wants to live a short life.

The threat of all three of these undesirable experiences hangs over the clone children, and Hailsham exists in order to evade that prospect, and make their childhoods in particular bearable through the absence of knowing the things which would destroy the students' happiness. Contrasts are made throughout the novel between the quality of life of those who have been to Hailsham and those who have not; and between the time where Hailsham and its mission were allowed to continue, and the grey, cheerless world after Hailsham.

As Tommy remarks to Kathy, the fact that, apart from Miss Lucy, there is a conspiracy of silence about what exactly donating and completing means does not prevent the children from absorbing enough hints and suggestions for them to have a general idea of what their future holds. Madame sees the myth of deferrals as a harmless dream, because so few students will ever try to obtain one for themselves. She evades the question of whether it is unfair or damaging to let the Ruths and the Tommys spend so much of their short lives misunderstanding how laughable and unrealistic the notion of extending their lives is.

Rumours at the Cottages suggest that veterans can secure a deferral in a minority of cases and then work in a shop or perhaps an office. Younger children at Hailsham dream of becoming film stars. To some extent, we all use dreams to cope with unpleasant or painful experiences; they are a legitimate form of escapism. The difference is that, as a young person reading and studying this novel, you are unlikely to have anything much worse than boredom to escape from! We feel that the children's increasingly desperate hopes- particularly after Hailsham- are both understandable and futile; a source of sadness for us as well as them.

Kathy is more realistic than Tommy or Ruth, perhaps because her self-sufficiency and her long experience as a carer make her sceptical about the prospect of avoiding the fate so many others have already suffered; she is less attached to the hope of a deferral than Tommy, and so she is less disturbed by losing that false hope in Chapter 22.

The importance of memories

The dying donor who wants to imagine he was at Hailsham too- he wants to use Kathy's stories of it as an anaesthetic- sets the tone in the first chapter; memories are important in the novel. For Kathy, they become all that connects her to her dead friends. Kathy believes that she will not lose her memories as she loses various organs during her own time as a donor.

It is through their detailed reminiscences of Hailsham that Ruth and Kathy are reconciled in Dover. Ruth tried to stress (to herself) that she was a mature person who had outgrown Hailsham, when she asked Keffers to dispose of her collection from her childhood.

The account of Ruth's behaviour towards Kathy throughout their time as children does not strike us as idyllic; Ruth was a bossy, controlling and manipulative child. At a distance of fifteen to twenty-five years, Kathy- who has made her peace with Ruth, who had died perhaps six years before Kathy narrates her story- treats Ruth generously, because these memories have become the remnants of what is now absent. There is no indication that any of the characters has photographs. Kathy has her tapes, and some lamps in her bedsit; Ruth's room in the recovery centre seemed to have nothing personal in it at all, and Tommy has his sketch books, and little else.

There is no mention of a funeral service for clones, a burial or a scattering of ashes. Once Hailsham has closed, or ceased to exist, there is nothing physical to connect Kathy's present with her past. Memories of the people who are now part of her past therefore become more important.

The children have never been allowed the opportunity to develop much of an identity of their own- just as a flock of sheep or a herd of cattle do not have their own suitcase or family photographs. For clones to accept their fates without resisting or complaining, it is helpful for them not to develop a sense of their own individuality, in case they then see themselves as "special" in a way which was not meant at Hailsham.

Perhaps what separates us from what we sometimes call "dumb animals" is the belief that they do not remember the past or have the capacity to think about the future. Kathy and her friends are treated as though they should have as little material as possible to fashion memories from; but, being fully human, they still do.

How to do exam questions

You must focus on the question, and you must plan your answer.

Proper planning can make a difference of several marks over a whole paper, and of at least one grade- sometimes more- because there is a world of difference between trying to show what you know in a random way, and producing a structured answer.

Your exam will allow you plenty of time to plan- it's included! But too many people don't bother to plan- they just start to write, because anxiety makes us want to make a start. These are the people whose time management in the exam will let them down. Their essays will be rambling and difficult to follow, and they will lose marks for being disorganised. Presumably you don't want to be in this group!

Planning your answer before you start guarantees two things—that you do answer the question, and stay relevant; and that you know when you've finished.

In your plan, you will organise what you are going to say. Then all you have to do is work steadily and concisely through it.

You must take the question apart and highlight the key words (often, that little word "How"). Your plan will give you an argument and a structure, and, by putting numbers against the points in your plan, in descending order of importance, you will already have organised your material in a sensible sequence.

The plan will lead you to a clear and convincing conclusion.

And it will tell you when to stop, because when you have covered all the points in your plan (crossing them out as you have finished writing each of them out), there will be no need to write anything more—no danger of adding that piece of irrelevant waffle which people who don't have a plan will be busy with next! They will be thinking "I'm not sure if I've finished—I'd better just write another paragraph or two", while you will be going on to the next question, with plenty of time to get another high mark.

As you write out the points in your plan, in your essay, check—constantly—that what you are writing is answering the question you have been set. If it isn't, leave it out.

Here are two sample essays. You can use them to work on the vital skill of planning. Why not take each essay apart?

See if you can reduce it to a plan on a single piece of paper, in the form of a spidergram. I think you'll find it a worthwhile thing to do.

Sample Essays

AQA style

How does Ishiguro present conflict?

Write about how he presents some conflicts; and how he uses conflicts to explore his ideas.

Plan- analyse the conflicts between Miss Lucy and Miss Emily; Tommy and Kathy; Ruth and Kathy; and relate them to Ishiguro's stated aims for the themes of the novel.

Suggested answer

The main areas of conflict are between Miss Lucy and the ethos of Hailsham; intermittently, between Kathy and Tommy; and, consistently, between Kathy and Ruth, whose friendship is troubled until they spend time together in Dover.

In Miss Lucy's opinion, it is wrong that the students have been given minimal information about the future course of their lives, because they are harbouring hopes and dreams (of becoming film stars, for example) which they will never have a chance to realise. She therefore sees no value in the stress on creativity which causes Tommy to be teased; she thinks that pretending that these children are valued like other, normal children, is a cruel deception. It is only in Chapter 22 that we find out the whole of the context for her sudden departure from Hailsham at the very end of Part 1 (Chapter 9). Miss Emily judged that Miss Lucy was "too theoretical", by which she means that telling the children everything would have destroyed them, because they would have been overcome with the same sense of worthlessness and distress which non-Hailsham students experienced.

Miss Lucy's humanity and Miss Emily's concern for the welfare of the children are too different in their practical application to be reconciled. Ishiguro has said that he wanted the novel to raise the question of how far we should try to protect our own children from the realities of an adult world which can be cruel and unpleasant, and at what point in their growing up we should stop sheltering them. Miss Lucy's role in the novel is to facilitate this theme.

Tommy finally acknowledges, as he faces his final donation and death, that he and Kathy have really always loved one another, from the earliest times, when she was concerned about his unhappy outbursts, on the football pitch, in art and in the classroom. We know that this is true, not just because they share a drive for discovering the truth, but because they have shared the joy of finding the replacement tape together, and because they had always communicated with complete honesty, in a way the other characters could not. They share their secrets -Tommy's art, and his theory about the true meaning of the Gallery, and Kathy's fears about her sex drive. They do not always deal with Ruth in a grown-up way, but they do behave relatively maturely with each other.

The way in which their relationship ends- it peters out, without dramatic avowals of undying love- reflects the poignant and uncomfortable fact that Tommy has an appointment to die, and that he does not want Kathy to be involved in the final tests and the regime of decline leading up to that. He has put on weight because he has become less able to be active, and presumably, as the fourth donation approaches, less medication is wasted on those who are soon to "complete", so their physical weakness becomes more evident. To have her as his carer to the very end would be too intimate. Tommy may feel that the experience would scar Kathy emotionally, and he would rather have her accept that, as Ruth had put it, death is their vocation, the end of their journey in life. Tommy's snappiness is understandable as a symptom of stress, but they manage to be reconciled thoroughly before he dies.

The same applies to Kathy and Ruth. Ruth had always been bossy towards Kathy (over her imaginary horses, the rules of chess, Miss Geraldine's guards). At the Cottages, Ruth's growing self-awareness and understanding that she has prevented, and continues to prevent, Tommy and Kathy from having the relationship they ought to have translates into cruelty towards Kathy; she tries to devalue and destroy her friendship with Tommy, by claiming that he would never have Kathy as a girlfriend. This sabotages their friendship, but it enables Ishiguro to motivate Ruth's desire for forgiveness before she dies.

Kathy is left to order her memories, of Hailsham and her dead friends. The later stages of her relationships with both Tommy and, particularly, Ruth show us Ishiguro working out the main theme he says he wanted the novel to raise- what matters to us most, when we know the time we have left is short.

WJEC style

What do you think of Kathy and the way she is presented in the novel?

Plan- her tone of voice/ Kathy as the narrator. Her reactions. Her behaviour. Her relationships with Tommy and Ruth. Her values and attitudes.

As the first-person narrator of the novel, Kathy is the key character. At the age of 31, she has seen the decline and deaths of many donors, including her own friends. At the end of the novel, she alone is left, gathering and clinging to her memories, as she faces the end of her own life.

Although she is an adult woman, Kathy's experience of love and intimacy is more on the level of a child's. Her descriptions of sex, and her understanding of it, are under-developed; she has never had a real opportunity to grasp its emotional power. However, she has a high degree of empathy, particularly towards Tommy.

Kathy is never self-indulgent- her daydream about Tommy coming back at the end of the narrative is her only indulgent moment. She abides by the rules, does her job with skill and dedication, and accepts her fate.

Perhaps she was too passive in allowing Ruth to dominate their friendship, and to keep her apart from Tommy for so long.

In chapter 22 Kathy asks some questions, which serve merely to break up what would otherwise be a long and unreadable monologue by Miss Emily. Kathy hardly reacts to the disappointing truth that there is no deferral- she is more composed than she expects herself to be. Madame is tearful; she feels sorry for Kathy. Kathy shows no self-pity. She herself almost never cries (only when she reveals to Tommy her motive for reading the porn magazines, in chapter 15, and at the end of the novel), and seems never even to raise her voice. Her final parting from Tommy is understated, and her account of Ruth's death at the end of chapter 19 is analytical, not emotional.

Kathy feels irritated and angry with Ruth, but she forgives her, and ultimately she sees Ruth as part of the trio or trinity which involves Tommy too. Kathy makes the interesting observation that she and Tommy always wanted knowledge (of the truth of their situation). They are mature enough to be reconciled to their own deaths.

At Hailsham, Kathy had supported Tommy, where others did not. Her friendship with Ruth, which started with the bossy business of Ruth's imaginary horses, and then Kathy's admittance to and expulsion from Miss Geraldine's guards, is one she allows Ruth to dominate. In part 2, Kathy understands Ruth's insecurity over Tommy (Ruth becomes more and more aware that they would have made a better couple) but she does not exploit it. She puts the needs of others before her own. She listens to the complaints of Laura, and to the fears of donors, when they need comfort, but she also knows that donors sometimes need to be treated less empathetically. We do not see much of this less empathetic style, but perhaps Kathy uses it more as a form of self-discipline than as a way of managing other people. At the end of chapter 14, Kathy is not afraid to confront Ruth- accusing her of talking nonsense- but her attempt to regulate Ruth's disappointment over her possible is unsuccessful. Ruth's self-indulgence contrasts with Kathy's self-control and adherence to the rules.

Kathy's sharp observation of other people's reactions, and her relative inattention to her own (she is not remotely self-obsessed), are a necessary part of being a first person narrator. Her tendency to be generous to others, in making allowances for their bad behaviour, is a striking characteristic. It reflects the fact that these young people are living under the shadow of death, and that their upbringing has lacked many of the influences (within a real family unit) which would enable them to relate to other people better.

The two attributes which define Kathy, as we read her, are humanity and courage. This is not accidental- it is what the novel is about. The strength and resilience of those qualities is never overstated in Kathy's narrative. She is better at observation than at description. Her range of similes, for example, is very narrow – made up, almost exclusively, of very basic comparisons about people acting on a stage.

Kathy is more reflective than Tommy and Ruth, and she has had a longer life than them, and therefore more time to analyse her own life and her friends' lives.

Appendix

Timelines

Back and forward through time

One of the most striking points about the way the novel is organised is its avoidance of a strictly chronological ordering of events. This makes it harder to read and understand. So let's look at it from both perspectives- the way we are asked to read, or decode, it, and the chronological sequence. Then we can judge what Ishiguro gains (and/or loses) by adopting the non-sequential approach.

The novel is set in England, in the late 1990s.

Kathy's recollections are almost entirely accurate, in that we are able to attach dates to the episodes she talks about. The occasional discrepancy is to be expected, and authentic; she describes so many events in such detail that her recall of the sequencing cannot be expected to be entirely reliable- it would be suspicious if it were that precise, and we might then suspect her of over-controlling her memories, and making her story up!

Timelines through Part One

Chapter 1

Kathy tells her story NOW; she is aged 31; she has been a carer for over 11 years, but will stop at the end of this year, in 8 months' time. We can suppose that this is therefore April 1998. She has been allowed to choose her donors for 6 years- since say 1992. Kathy was "born" (or cloned) in 1967. She left Hailsham at the age of 16 in 1983. Ruth was the third or fourth donor she chose- in early 1992. Kathy will then have been a carer from the start of 1987.

The donor so interested in Hailsham was alive, and died, in 1990.

Kathy was in the Juniors, i.e. at Hailsham, from the age of 4- in 1971.

Tommy's football match is when Kathy was 13- in 1980.

So the action in this chapter dates from 1998 – 1993 – 1980.

Chapter 2

This chapter starts with Kathy and Tommy talking soon after the football incident- so it is set in 1980. Then there is an account of Tommy's problems in the period which follows. After two months, Kathy raises the unfairness about some people's behaviour towards Tommy, in the dormitory. Exchange Tokens are in use.

The narrative switches to Kathy and Ruth in Dover, in the summer of 1992, after Ruth's first donation. Satellite dishes form part of the skyline (Sky TV launched in 1989). Kathy recalls that they would use tokens to buy the poems from other pupils in their own year at the age of 9- in 1976- and she talks about their understanding of poetry at the age of 11.

Kathy's thoughts revert to the scene in 1980, and Tommy's juvenile elephant painting in the summer of that year, when they were aged 13; then she recalls a conversation with Tommy about his ongoing difficulties at Hailsham, in 1993 or 1994.

Tommy supplies the details of his 1980 conversation with Miss Lucy, in which she told him that it was fine not to be creative.

So the action dates from 1980 - 1993 - 1980.

Chapter 3

Kathy and Tommy continue their 1980 discussion the same day, at the duck pond; it is in October. Tommy recounts more of what Miss Lucy had said to him; that he was a very good student, and that the children were not being taught enough about the reality of their futures.

Kathy remembers being aware of rumours about the Gallery at the age of 5 or 6- perhaps in 1973.

She recalls the scaring of Madame, when the children were aged 8- in the autumn of 1975.

So the action dates from 1980 – 1973 – 1975.

Chapter 4

The narrative returns to the duck pond discussion in 1980, and then goes on to a recollection of a class discussion of Exchange Tokens, in Junior 4, when they were ten- in 1977. Kathy is certain of this, but it contradicts the information in chapter 2 that tokens were already in use when they were 9. Chapter 4 is unambiguous in saying that tokens were introduced when Kathy was ten.

That same year, Miss Lucy is asked why the art goes to the Gallery; she will not explain, but says there is a good reason for it. The memory of that lesson in the library comes back to Kathy in her discussion with Tommy at the pond- although that is three years later.

Kathy sees Miss Emily behaving in an apparently bizarre way in Senior 3- when she is aged 13.

Kathy recalls her first encounters with Ruth at the age of five or six- in 1973- and then two years later- in 1975- and Ruth's plan to have secret guards to protect Miss Geraldine.

So the action dates mainly from 1977, then 1980, then 1975, then 1973.

Chapter 5

This continues the secret guards project, until Ruth expels Kathy from it- in 1975 or possibly 1976.

The last part of the chapter deals with the incident of Ruth's pencil case, three years later- when the children were 11 or 12, in 1978 or 1979.

Chapter 6

This chapter continues from the previous one- Ruth no longer carries the pencil case with her. Kathy repairs their relationship when she protects Ruth from Midge A's questions about the origin of the pencil case. A month later, Kathy loses her treasured tape of songs by Judy Bridgewater, and Ruth investigates its disappearance, before giving Kathy what she thinks will be an effective substitute.

The middle of the chapter deals with the origins of the idea that rubbish and lost property went to Norfolk, and Kathy's recent reminiscences on this with Tommy. By the age of 12 or 13, they will have had stopped believing this- in 1979/80. Madame sees Kathy singing and dancing to the tape; within weeks, it vanishes. The failed search implies that the guardians have removed it, because it glamourises smoking.

Kathy relates, briefly, Tommy's suggestion that Madame has mind-reading powers- this is from a conversation late in 1980; the point that the tape had gone missing a couple of years earlier confirms the Madame episode as being from 1978.

Marge's embarrassing questioning of Miss Lucy over whether she had ever smoked leads to the pressing of Marge's face against the window in chapter 5- in 1975/6. Kathy's note that the children were now aged 9/10 is consistent with 1976.

Because of the importance of the tape, this chapter has a stronger focus than previous chapters on a single period – 1978 or 1979.

Ruth's first donation was in 1991, and she is now dead, in 1998; she died in 1992, at the age of 25.

Chapter 7

This chapter opens by telling us that the next three chapters- to the end of part 1 of the novel- will deal with the later years at Hailsham, from the ages of 13 to 16- from 1980 to 1983.

Miss Lucy had a lesson which turned to talk of accidents and suicide, in late 1979. Then, when Kathy was 15, and in their final autumn at Hailsham - in 1982- Miss Lucy uses the chatter about future careers to impress on the class that they have no freedom of choice, and will die prematurely.

Kathy recalls Miss Emily's sex lectures when she was about 13- in 1980. That was the year of Tommy's difficulties, and his gashed elbow.

The final paragraph of the chapter introduces Kathy's encounter with Miss Lucy in Room 22, during the final summer at Hailsham- 1983.

Chapter 8

The narrative records Miss Lucy's apparently manic behaviour in room 22, which leaves Kathy with a presentiment that something ominous or significant was about to occur. Also, a few days later, Miss Lucy had a conversation with Tommy which unsettled him; this cannot be the same as the art conversation, which had been in 1980.

The detail of this conversation emerges, from Tommy, in the second half of chapter 9.

Chapter 8 focuses entirely on the summer of 1983.

Chapter 9

This chapter brings Kathy's time at Hailsham to an end. Ruth and Tommy are in a relationship. Culture Briefings prepare the children for dealing with the various professions they will encounter in the wider world.

Miss Lucy has left Hailsham, suddenly. These are the children's final weeks there, too- still in 1983.

Overview- structure of Part One

The structure of the chapters becomes more chronologically coherent, in chapters 7-9. The more chaotic pattern in the earlier chapters serves to underline the distinction Kathy makes at the start of chapter 7; until the age of 13, life seemed enchanted and glowing; from 13 to 16, it became different, as the children began to develop a sense that their future would be much less enjoyable than their lives to date.

On one level, the various episodes at Hailsham are like school stories- straightforward tales of friendships and bullying. But, although Kathy's language is often childish and clumsy- it is less educated than she is herself- Ishiguro manages to chart the emotional development from childhood to adolescence. He leaves us in no doubt that his main characters are fully human, even though they are somewhat handicapped by their lack of a family as the basis or template for successful adult relationships. They are, effectively, each other's family.

Ishiguro has achieved something difficult here; he has convinced us that Kathy and the others have grown up programmed and conditioned to accept their terrible fate. The consequences of rebelling against it are only hinted at, and they are all the more sinister for that-

disfigurement and death in the woods, or perhaps an encounter with an electrified fence, such as Miss Lucy hints at in chapter 7, where suicide is not presented as an option.

In real life, people living under an extended death sentence would need to be guarded tightly if they were not to do desperate harm to themselves and/or other people. Ishiguro simply makes his children ultra-conformists, so that we feel that there is no possibility of such a breakout. Even at the age of 16, there is a degree of naivete about them which does just enough to convince us that the clones accept their eventual fate, because they have not developed a sense of its complete and outrageous unfairness.

Timelines through Part Two

Chapter 10

The Hailsham students arrived at the Cottages in the summer of 1983; their essays were, in theory, to be a two-year project.

Within a year, Kathy is taking driving lessons (late in 1984). The former students from Hailsham did indeed stay there for two years.

Autumn 1983- a major row with Ruth.

Chapter 11

Autumn 1983, with a short flash forward to Ruth in Dover – in 1992.

Chapter 12

The first winter at the Cottages is almost over, so it is early 1984- the theory that Rodney has seen Ruth's possible; a flashback to the origin of Ruth's dream future.

Chapter 13

The Norfolk day trip is in early 1984. Deferrals are talked about.

Chapter 14

Ruth's lies over deferrals; the sighting of the possible.

Chapter 15

The same day; that afternoon; Tommy and Kathy find the tape; they discuss the gallery and Kathy's sex urges; the return journey.

Chapter 16

Spring 1984. More veterans are leaving to start their training as carers. Two people from the Hailsham group of 8 leave in April for training (Alice F and Gordon C).

Summer 1984. Ruth is now denying remembering things from Hailsham. The narrative of the argument Kathy has with her in the bus shelter starts and breaks off.

Earlier (a few weeks) - Ruth discovers the replacement tape in Kathy's bedroom; they discuss Tommy's drawings.

Several days later- in the churchyard- Ruth tells Tommy that Kathy thinks his art is bad.

Chapter 17

The unfinished essays seem less important with time passing. Ruth and Tommy have grown quite distant.

Back to the bus shelter story. Ruth tells Kathy that Tommy is too choosy or selective for Kathy ever to be his girlfriend.

Soon Kathy applies to start her training, and soon after that she leaves. This is in the later part of 1984. When Kathy speaks of two years at the Cottages, she means a large part of 1983 and most of 1984.

Overview- structure of Part Two

Chapters 10-17 are coherent because the Cottages are in the background. The trip to Norfolk is planned in Chapter 12, and narrated in Chapters 13-15. It establishes the relationship Tommy has with Ruth as much less durable than the one he ought to have had with Kathy; he is at fault for not making the careful choice he knew he needed to, in Chapter 9.

Chapters 16 and 17 show us Ruth behaving so badly that her friendship with Kathy breaks down. It cannot continue as it was when they were younger, but Ruth's insecurity over the fact that Tommy had replaced Kathy's lost tape without telling her about it leads her to sabotage Kathy's potential relationship with Tommy. Ruth regrets this and tries to atone for it, in Chapter 19.

Timelines through Part Three

Chapter 18

Kathy's awkward meeting with Laura takes place seven years after they had left the Cottages, so this chapter seems to be set in late 1991, in a wintry wind. Ruth had still been a carer a few years ago.

Now there is a rumour that Ruth had a really bad time over her first donation. Kathy will therefore start to make arrangements- within a few weeks or months- to become Ruth's carer, but this starts to work only after their initial awkwardness has subsided.

Kathy has only had the privilege of choosing her donors since about the start of 1992, and Ruth is among the earlier donors she becomes responsible for (Chapter 1). Ruth's first donation appears to have been almost at the end of 1991.

Laura and Kathy both know that Hailsham has closed. Rumours that it was to be sold immediately had circulated in 1990.

Kathy first goes to see Ruth at the Dover recovery centre, probably early in 1992. This is two months after Ruth's first donation. Kathy has arranged to become her carer- but for some time they don't get on, because Ruth thinks Kathy wants some kind of revenge. Then they plan to see the boat. Ruth has not seen Tommy since they were all at the Cottages. Their relationship had not lasted beyond 1984.

Chapter 19

The boat excursion is the centrepiece of this part of the novel, rather as the trip to Norfolk had been in Part 2. They collect Tommy in the afternoon, on a dull, cool day; perhaps towards the end of winter, possibly in February.

Chrissie had died during her second donation. Kathy had seen her in a clinic on only one occasion.

Tommy never learned to drive and had a very short time as a carer.

Ruth had been a carer for 5 years, from 1986.

Kathy and Ruth make the return trip to Dover that evening.

Some weeks later, the summer of 1992 is approaching. Kathy and Ruth can now talk more openly, and reminisce, for several months. Ruth dies 3 days after her second donation.

Chapter 20

Almost exactly a year after the boat excursion, Kathy becomes Tommy's carer; so the setting is early in 1992. The Spring and early summer of 1992 follow. This is not long after Tommy's third donation. Towards the end of the summer, in early or mid- September – there is heavy rain- Kathy has been to Littlehampton, to check that Ruth had the correct address for Madame; Kathy and Tommy go there together during the following week.

Chapters 21 and 22

The visit itself takes place at 6pm.

Hailsham had lost all its sponsors in just over a year, in 1988/9.

Kathy drives on the journey back in the dark. Tommy's outburst in the field takes place.

Chapter 23

This Chapter is set in October 1992. Tommy's focus on Kathy weakens, as there is no deferral and his fourth donation cannot be escaped from. The notice for it duly arrives.

There is no indication of how much advance notice of the fourth and final donation is given, or how long donors are given to recuperate after the third donation.

Kathy's final visit to Tommy is therefore in December 1992. We can assume that he completes/dies in the earlier part of 1993.

Kathy's final thoughts return to her immediate future- the remainder of 1998. When we appreciate that it is already five years since Tommy died- and that she has been alone since then- we can appreciate more readily how tired she feels. The novel ends with her own outburst of grief in a field in Norfolk- two weeks after she had heard that Tommy had died. That is, once more, a windy day- perhaps in March or April 1993.

Overview – structure of Part Three

The final part of the novel covers a period of 18 months, which ends in the first part of 1993- five years before Kathy tells her story to the unnamed carer/clone to whom she addresses her narrative.

The focus is on Ruth's quest for forgiveness, then her death, and finally on resolving the mystery of the deferrals, although we sense it is too late for this to be a realistic prospect. Once that escapist dream has died- "The Great Escape" for Tommy and Kathy- there is not much left to tell; just Tommy's death, and Kathy's isolation, as she faces the same grim path herself.

Most autobiographies will follow an upward curve, from childhood and education to adulthood, achievement and some degree of happiness and satisfaction. Kathy's story reverses this arc, so that Hailsham is, looking back, a charmed time, followed by a life which begins to reflect the dark and cheerless landscape at and beyond the Cottages.

The focus on a narrator's thoughts and memories is a "modernist" style for a novel. We have the sense that, before she loses her health and her clarity of mind and purpose, Kathy wants to create a record of what will not otherwise survive- an oral history of life at the closed and vanished Hailsham, which is, indeed, as Madame puts it, benign but unable to survive the pressures of a society which is ruthless in its pursuit of applying medical advances.

To us, the readers of the novel, the non-residents, Hailsham is not that- it is no more than a service station on the motorway of the newer outside world, with its cruelty and its lack of conscience in putting the clones to death. In the end, after having to let go of all her friends, whom she has outlived, Kathy hopes that her memories of Hailsham will somehow form a shared experience which survives or transcends death, so that those memories will be like her feelings about her tape; they will represent something comforting and emotional, which will never let go of her, even though she has to let go of it.

Chronology

We cannot be absolutely sure of every detail of this, because the time when Kathy starts her story is imprecise. If we assume- quite reasonably- that this is April 1998, and that Kathy will have stopped being a carer at the end of 1998, the chronology is as follows-

1967   Kathy born.

1971   Attends Hailsham.

1973   Rumours of the Gallery.

1973-5   Kathy's early friendship with Ruth.

1975   The crowding around Madame.

1975   Ruth expels Kathy from Miss Geraldine's guards.

1978   Madame sees Kathy with her pillow and her tape.

1978-9   Ruth's pencil case. Kathy's tape goes missing.

1980   Tommy's football match; his injured elbow; his elephant painting. Miss Lucy tells him art   does not matter. The lesson about being told and not told. Miss Emily's sex lectures. Miss Emily rehearses her presentations for the outside world.

1983   Kathy leaves Hailsham. Ruth and Tommy are a couple. They all go to the Cottages.

1984   Trip to Cromer. Ruth's pursuit of her original, from whom she was cloned; deferral rumours; Kathy's replacement tape.

1984   Kathy leaves the Cottages; starts carer training and driving lessons after Ruth tells her Tommy will never consider her as his girlfriend. Ruth and Tommy drift apart.

1986-1991   Ruth is a carer; does not see Tommy.

1987   Kathy starts working as a carer.

1988?   Morningdale scandal.

1990   Hailsham closes.

1991   Kathy meets Laura. Ruth has had a bad first donation.

1992   Kathy becomes her carer. Ruth dies three days after her second donation.

1992   Kathy becomes Tommy's carer, after his third donation. Their relationship starts. Late in the year they visit Madame and Miss Emily. There are no deferrals. Tommy receives notice of his fourth (final and fatal) donation late in 1992; it is presumably due early in 1993.

Tommy dies. Kathy continues as a carer for a further five years, resisting Tommy's advice before he died.

1999   Kathy's donations will begin.

A note on names

The children at Hailsham generally share the initial of their Christian name with others-

Amanda C, Arthur H, Alexander J, Annette B

Carole H, Christopher H, Christopher C, Charlotte F, Cynthia E, Christy

Gary B, Gordon, Graham K

Harry C, Hannah

Jackie , Jenny B, Jenny C

Marge K, Moira B, Midge A, Matilda, Martha H

Peter B, Peter N, Polly T, Patricia C, Peter J

Roy C, Rob D, Roger D, Reggie D, Ruth

Sharon D, Sylvia B, Susie K, Sylvie C

This leaves only Laura, Tommy D and Kathy H who do not share an initial with someone else; perhaps they are original, more original or individual than Ruth? Ishiguro is giving them a special status by separating their names and individualising them in this way.

I wonder whether this roll-call of names at Hailsham resembles in any way that of a normal school, in real life. It reads as if many letters of the alphabet have disappeared altogether- only a third of the alphabet is left; the rest has already been wiped out.

This uniformity of names does not transfer to the Cottages.

The guardians- Mr Chris, Jack, Roger, George, Robert; Miss Lucy, Eileen, Emily, Geraldine- have unremarkable names, except that Lucy is derived from the Latin word LUX, or light. Miss Lucy tries to enlighten the students about their futures, but she is immediately removed. They are to be kept in the dark, for their own comfort and protection.

Gavin Smithers is a private tutor, covering Broadway, Chipping Campden and the North Cotswolds. He has an English degree from Oxford University, and a passion for helping others to discover the joy and satisfaction of great literature.

And finally ...if there's anything you're not sure about and your teacher can't help, contact the author –
grnsmithers@hotmail.co.uk

Gavin's Guides are short books packed with insight. Their key aim is to help you raise your grade!

Understanding Arthur Miller's All My Sons. Understanding J.B. Priestley's An Inspector Calls. Understanding George Orwell's Animal Farm. Understanding William Golding's Lord of the Flies. Understanding Charles Dickens' Great Expectations. Understanding John Steinbeck's Of Mice and Men. Understanding Emily Dickinson's Set Poems. Understanding Edward Thomas' Set Poems. Understanding Harper Lee's To Kill A Mockingbird. Understanding Andrew Marvell's Cromwell & Eulogy Poems. Understanding Poems of the Decade for A level Edexcel Poetry.

Printed in Great Britain
by Amazon